How Can I Believe What Can't Be Believed? (Genesis 1-3)

Questions for a Logical Mind

MATT W. LEACH

WESTBOW
PRESS®
A DIVISION OF THOMAS NELSON
& ZONDERVAN

WestBow Press books may be ordered through booksellers or by contacting:

WestBow Press
A Division of Thomas Nelson & Zondervan
1663 Liberty Drive
Bloomington, IN 47403
www.westbowpress.com
1 (866) 928-1240

Because of the dynamic nature of the Internet, any web addresses or links contained in this book may have changed since publication and may no longer be valid. The views expressed in this work are solely those of the author and do not necessarily reflect the views of the publisher, and the publisher hereby disclaims any responsibility for them.

Any people depicted in stock imagery provided by Thinkstock are models, and such images are being used for illustrative purposes only.
Certain stock imagery © Thinkstock.

Interior image by Doring Kindersley: James Mann / Chris Williams

Scripture quotations taken from the Amplified® Bible (AMP), Copyright © 2015 by The Lockman Foundation Used by permission. www.Lockman.org

Scripture quotations are from the ESV® Bible (The Holy Bible, English Standard Version®), copyright © 2001 by Crossway, a publishing ministry of Good News Publishers. Used by permission. All rights reserved.

Scripture quotations marked (KJV) are from the King James Version.

Scripture quotations marked (NIV) are taken from the Holy Bible, New International Version®, NIV®. Copyright © 1973, 1978, 1984, 2011 by Biblica, Inc.™ Used by permission of Zondervan. All rights reserved worldwide. www.zondervan.com The "NIV" and "New International Version" are trademarks registered in the United States Patent and Trademark Office by Biblica, Inc.™

Scripture quotations marked (PHP) are taken from The New Testament in Modern English, copyright 1958, 1959, 1960 J.B. Phillips and 1947, 1952, 1955, 1957 The Macmillian Company, New York. Used by permission. All rights reserved.

ISBN: 978-1-5127-7598-3 (sc)
ISBN: 978-1-5127-7599-0 (e)

Library of Congress Control Number: 2017902231

Print information available on the last page.

WestBow Press rev. date: 03/24/2017

Contents

Other Titles by Matt W Leach

You've Got to Know the Territory Before You Pray

Peter, the Professor and the Blue Orb Time Machine

Preface

I was talking with a friend about some of the biblical stories that seemed impossible to believe. The more we talked, the more apparent it became that he wasn't listening to me but was repeating many opinions and beliefs he held and was defending. Many of his beliefs and opinions were based on flawed science; this was compounded by a lack of understanding of the literal meaning of the Hebrew and Greek words. The Hebrew and Greek words are meant to be understood literally unless they specifically say otherwise. Too often, people assume that words are symbolical or metaphorical. That is especially true today when modern science is unwrapping new knowledge that makes old scientific beliefs seem antiquated or even wrong.

As I pondered this, I thought someone should write a book to help people like my friend uncover the truth. No sooner had I thought that when the words rose up from the Holy Spirit within me saying, "You write it!" So I have written it. I don't have all the answers, so don't look for them here.

Only one thing is required when you read this book—do so with an open mind and seek to understand what I'm writing. Be logical; think logically. Let your mind be stimulated to think in ways you haven't thought before. Be open to logical possibilities you had not considered before.

INTRODUCTION

The Star Car

Imagine yourself in another world, another dimension, another reality. In your driveway sits your car. While very old, some say ancient, its design is futuristic. Its two doors hinged at the top give the appearance of a gull's wings when they're open. Its iridescent, pearl-grey color is accented with silver trim. A car just like yours sits in every driveway. As has everyone else, you have learned to drive your car to work, the store—anywhere—and return home.

You have been told many times—indeed, you've attended many lectures that taught, even preached, that what you're doing with your car is what a car does and that's all it does. However, as you sit in your car and look at the console and at panels that look like they could be doors that slide open but don't, you get the gnawing suspicion that your car is designed to do more. Stories, or myths as some would say, are told that declare that it actually it is a star car designed to travel to planets.

This suspicion grows as you study the manufacturer's handbook. Admittedly, the handbook is a little difficult to understand; it too is very old and its language archaic. The experts all seem to agree that the car is doing all it was designed to do. True, ancient copies of the manufacturer's handbook say others drove them into space. However, experts remind us, that was only a metaphor and that the first readers of the handbook understood it as such. There is no evidence to suggest that it actually happened.

That's another thing that bothers you. Countless scholars can tell you all about the manufacturer's handbook. There are experts on the age of the manuscripts, experts on whether it was written by one author or many, experts on the meaning of words—but there are no scholars, no experts who can tell you how to do what the handbook says to do!

As time passes, your dissatisfaction with all the expert opinions about your car grows. The time comes when you begin a quest of your own. You want to know if your car is more than just a mode of transportation. You want to know if there is truth in the ancient stories. How can you find out?

First, you temporarily set aside everything the scholars have taught on the matter. You will study the manufacturer's handbook as if reading it for the first time. You will assume the writer is saying what he meant and meant what he wrote. If what is written is a figure of speech, the writer will say so. If not, you will assume the literal meaning. Wherever words are archaic or meanings have changed, you will restate them in today's language.

Second, you will expand your mind. You read things that challenge you to think big and envision the impossible as though it were possible. You seek out like-minded people who also believe there is more to their cars. You will share what you have learned and your ideas of what has yet to be learned.

Having set out on this quest, a day comes when you're sitting in your car with the manufacturer's handbook in hand studying the console when you see something you've overlooked. You can't believe your eyes. You read it again and then you do it. As you turn the ignition key on, you reach out with your other hand and touch a button you had always assumed was only a decoration. The panels on the console slide open. Before you are all the switches, controls, guidance systems, and indicator lights of a star car!

You spend the next weeks and months learning. The manufacturer's handbook you thought so outdated and ancient has become a new book. Following its instructions, you learn how to accelerate you star car for liftoff. You learn how to overcome gravity and soar out into space. You learn how to rise above the sun and explore vistas of opportunity undreamed of before.

Today in Our Reality

If you were to take a survey today to discover how many people would like to own the star car described above, I don't think you'd find many. We're too comfortable where we are and with what we have; we're too comfortable with our opinions. The lives we're living even with their miseries and challenges may be far from ideal, but at least they're familiar; we've found ways to cope.

This comfortableness with things as they are is one reason people have difficulty with the Bible. Yet deep down in the back of our minds like an irritation we can't scratch, there's the suspicion we actually do have a star car and can soar above the sun.

Sometimes, we hear people say something like, "I was meant for more than this." It is a heart cry for life to have meaning and purpose. Life has to be more than eat, drink, and be merry because tomorrow we'll die. It may be that deep inside our minds, we wonder if there is any truth in the Bible's claims that we can live a victorious life now and continue that victorious life in heaven. If for no other reason than to settle things in our minds, we need to answer the questions, Is the Bible a collection of stories or truth? Was humanity created for a purpose? Does my life have a purpose, a goal?

The temptation we must temporarily set aside is that of assuming the

Bible is nothing but a collection of stories, even myths. Many people say that's all it is, but to assume that is dishonest. However, I can understand why we are tempted to assume that. It has been preached to us in school, churches, colleges, the media—everywhere—that the earth is billions of years old and that we are the product of evolution having evolved by chance from primordial scum. We are told the earth couldn't have been created in six days as the Bible claims. That's part of our hang-up with the Bible.

We find ourselves asking, if the Genesis story of creation isn't true, how can we believe or trust or know if any of the rest of the Bible is true? That's a tough question because it has always been believed that there was no empirical, provable evidence. We easily forget or overlook the fact that there is also no empirical, provable evidence for the theories and opinions that have been accepted as truth. We want proof that can be tested in the lab. At the least, theories must not violate or ignore scientific laws, but we accept as true theories that violate and ignore scientific laws. Discussing those flaws is not the purpose of this book though I'll mention a few in passing.

Instead, while you are studying this book set aside all you've been taught, all you've thought, all your opinions, and start from scratch. Keep on pretending that you own a star car and that you've just discovered that there's more to the manufacturer's handbook than you had ever imagined. To help you do this, we'll examine the Bible in an unusual way—we'll stand back as it were and look at the its story as a whole.

Seen from this perspective, the story the Bible tells is strange. It almost reads like science fiction from a galaxy far, far away. It's a story that many say is true, but it will sound like the strangest tale you've ever heard. Many will tell you the story isn't true. They can't prove it isn't true, but they will say it anyway because they don't want to believe it.

It is the story about the greatest Sorcerer of all—not a weaver of spells or someone who uses magic and potions and stuff but the ultimate source of all power who needs no spells or magic or potions and stuff. The story is told in the only book the Sorcerer says is authentic. So the questions are, Is this source really true? Or is it a tall tale? Or even a myth? There are many voices saying the book conflicts with science, that it is just a collection of myths and tales and some wisdom literature.

If you have wondered, if you have asked those questions, you might find this little book to be stimulating and thought provoking. It will lead you on a quest of discovery. It may take you down paths you've not gone down before. It won't give you answers, but it will help you ask the right questions. Our method of inquiry will be the one prescribed by the Sorcerer himself, who keeps saying, "Look at the facts!"[1]

Is the story true? Is it a tall tale? Is it a myth? You'll have to make up your own mind on that. You will find space at the end of each chapter for you to jot down your thoughts and questions. In many places, I have chosen the path of the storyteller to fill in the gaps in the story to make it more interesting. I haven't knowingly altered any fact. For example, it makes the story of the Fall more interesting when we add the thoughts that might have passed through Satan's mind and through Adam and Eve's minds as near as we can guess from the details we're given. That's what a storyteller does. But he doesn't change the facts.

CHAPTER 1

The Incredible Story

As we calculate it, time is nothing more than a sum of the 365.25 times the earth rotates on its axis for each orbit it makes around the sun. Logically then, if you don't have an earth or a sun, you don't have time!

This is important to consider because the story the Bible tells is an epic drama that began before time. It tells how things were before there was evil. Then it tells how evil came to be, and finally, it tells how evil will end. All the events of creation and the rebellion of Lucifer are linked together in the following narrative. All the recorded facts are unaltered.

The Roll Call of Heaven

The Bible's story of Creation seems at first to be like science fiction as in a story that's too far-fetched to be believed. We could leave it at that except for something that happens at the end of the story. For that reason, we'll take time to repeat the biblical story of Creation.

The story begins before there was a sun or an earth to circle it. It begins so long ago that time didn't exist. There was no universe, no stars, no planets—nothing. Nothing except a Being without beginning or end. A Being who said of himself that "HE WAS, and IS, and EVER SHALL BE."[1] Our minds are conditioned to think that everything has a beginning. Not so, this Being tells us.

This Being was and is by nature loving and kind—the epitome of goodness. Logically, he couldn't have done what he was about to do if he hadn't been! The reason is simple. Evil is a destroyer, not a creator. Good and evil can't coexist because they are opposites and would cancel each other out. Logically, it was because this Being was good and because evil did not exist that he could create.

When asked his name, he said his name is I AM (Exodus 3:14). He also said that he was One and there was no other (Isaiah 44:6–8). Even though he was One, he also existed as three. How that can be so is a mystery he has not explained. In fact, there is much about himself he has not explained. If you ask him, "Where did you come from?" he will say, "I always was and am and will be" (Revelation 1:8). "Are there others besides you?" we ask. His answer is, "I am One and there is no other" (Isaiah 45:5).

There is one thing we know for certain about I Am. We know he is a creator. He alone has the power to create. According to what is written in his book, he and he alone created all things (John 1:3; Colossians 1:16)). He tells us the way he created was to make something out of nothing. He did this by speaking words. He conceived the thing he wanted and then called it into existence with a word, and the thing suddenly existed.[2] First, there was nothing, and then there was something. The universe came into being by his spoken word: "By the word of the LORD were the heavens made, their starry host by the breath of his mouth" (Psalm 33:6 NIV).

How much did he create? We don't know. Perhaps he created a vast number of galaxies and star systems. Perhaps he created only one. It is known that he lives and has his throne in in a place he calls highest heaven.[3] There was a place called Eden, the garden of God, which may no longer exist. There was a holy mountain with red sapphires that gleamed like flames of fire.[4] When he finished creating, he said of all that he had created, "It is very good."

He also created companies of beings called angels that numbered in the tens of thousands and thousands of thousands.[5] The angels had bodies that looked similar to ours, and they ate food similar to ours.[6] Some had wings and could fly. They may, though it is not said, have lived on worlds like ours. What did the angels do? Why were there so many? We can only speculate because little is said; the word *angel* means messenger, one who is sent.

Their method of travel is unknown with the exception of a description in one place of a strange-looking, wheel-within-a-wheel spacecraft.[7] Elsewhere is mention of a spacecraft called a chariot that could ascend above earth.[8] Angelic beings are not normally visible to the human eye though there are firsthand reports in the Bible of encounters between angels and humans. In one place, it says that they had horses, chariots, and swords.[9]

The multitudes of angels were arranged in divisions; each division ruled over a part of creation and was governed by a ruling archangel, and the other angels were organized in a descending order of authority. Their order of rank was like that of an army.[10] One archangel was named Michael (who is like God).[11] A second was named Lucifer (light bearer, bright, and morning star).[12] A third may have been named Gabriel (mighty of God).[13]

We are told that the archangel Lucifer was the greatest and most magnificent. His beauty, wisdom, and greatness were unsurpassed. He was blameless and perfect in all his ways from the instant he was created. Not a tinge of evil was to be found in him because there could be no tinge or spot of evil in anything God had made.

Apparently, he led the worship in heaven.[14] He was created with a voice so beautiful and mesmerizing that it lifted heaven's worship to the highest level of praise to the enjoyment and ecstasy of all. His rulership is thought to have included at least earth, where his throne was, and the heavens surrounding the planet.[15]

Worship under Lucifer's leadership was a delight for the angels. It was a joy unspeakable and full of glory not because it was demanded or required but because it was what they wanted to do. I Am was a joy giver and took delight in the joy of his creation. It delighted him to see the waves of joy as Lucifer led the angels in worship. He himself danced and jumped and shouted for joy at the joy his creation experienced.[16] He was a happy Creator.

Lucifer Became Intoxicated with Himself

The grateful angelic host was quick to lavish praise and admiration on Lucifer for his inspired leadership. Because his wisdom was so great, the angels also loved to be in his presence and listen to his words. As Lucifer basked in this praise and adoration, the unthinkable slowly began to happen—he began to take pride in his beauty and wisdom.[17] The more highly he thought of himself, the less highly he thought of God. He grew discontented with how God ruled. He may have begun to look on God's dancing and joyous demeanor as a sign of weakness or even flippancy.

Lucifer, in love with himself, began to think he was at least God's equal if not even greater than God. Lust for power mingled with pride began to consume him. The light in him began to dim into darkness forcing him to masquerade as an angel of light.[18] That degeneration is how the dark force of evil, the dark enemy that seeks to overthrow all other powers and rule the universe, came into being.

> You were in Eden, God's garden. You were dressed in splendor, your robe studded with jewels: Carnelian, peridot, and moonstone, beryl, onyx, and jasper, Sapphire, turquoise, and emerald, all in settings of engraved gold. A robe was prepared for you the same day you were created. You were the anointed cherub. I placed you on the mountain of God. You strolled in magnificence among the stones of fire. From the day of your creation you were sheer perfection … and then imperfection— evil!—was detected in you.[19]

The story has turned from one of peace, love, and joy to an epic story of the battle between good and evil. Lucifer fell deeper into darkness. In that darkness, a plan took shape in his mind. He would take God's place. "Am I not like God?" he asked, and the third of the angelic host under him answered, "Yes!" He began declaring, "I will exalt my throne above the stars of God. I will sit on the mount of the congregation in the sides of the north. I will ascend above the heights of the clouds. I will make myself like the Most High" (Isaiah 14:13).

Rebellion consumed his every thought though he hid it well. This archangel, this ruler of a third of the angels, this most perfect of all the angels, began to sow seeds of rebellion in the hearts and minds of all the ruling angels under his command. Perhaps he promised them rewards and promotions that would be more worthy of their talents than they would receive from God.

The rebellion spread until thousands and thousands of angels, a third of the angelic host, joined his rebellion. When all was ready, when all his forces were fully instructed and prepared, Lucifer led his forces in an attack on the throne of God. What were their weapons? Brute force would not have worked; they were outnumbered two to one. No, this war called for powerful weapons. It might have been that Lucifer thought by merely speaking words as God spoke words at creation he would achieve his goal. But he was not God, and his words were without power. What weapons he then chose to use we don't know.

Perhaps the heavens were filled with blinding explosions—a profusion of greens, reds, yellows, whites, and blues mixed in fireworks gone mad. Perhaps thunderous noise and explosions shook heaven's foundations. When the smoke cleared, it was not God who had been defeated—it was Lucifer. Lucifer's planet was devastated, shrouded in icky, slimy darkness.

Lucifer had lost all he had had. He was an archangel without a country. Wrenched out of his hands forever was the place he once walked and over which he once ruled. The angels he had groomed to fight his war were held in chains in the thick gloom of utter darkness awaiting their doom.[20] Only a few of his coconspirators were left. Earth's inhabitants who had followed their master in rebellion became demons shorn of their bodies.

Rage filled Lucifer. He may have lost the battle, but the war wasn't over. He was determined to win. He still had a few powerful angels and multitudes of demons. He would get his kingdom back. He would ascend above the throne of God. He took upon himself a new name. He would be Satan, adversary and diabolic slanderer. All he needed was to get his planet back. But how? God had robbed him, so he thought, of the ability to re-create his planet, or create a different planet, or speak things into existence. Considering himself smarter than God, he would wait until God did something foolish. Then he would strike.

A New Beginning

All the above was pre-history and pre-time. Time as we know it was about to begin. It came to pass that once again I Am created. His spirit hovered over the ravaged planet that lay in chaotic darkness. Genesis 1:2 tells us that the earth had become a wasteland, void and empty. Darkness covered it.[21] In a vision, Jeremiah witnessed the destruction.

> I beheld the earth, and, lo, it was without form, and void; and the heavens, and they had no light. I beheld the mountains, and, lo, they trembled, and all the hills moved lightly. I beheld, and, lo, there was no man, and all the birds of the heavens were fled. I beheld, and, lo, the fruitful place was a wilderness, and all the cities thereof were broken down at the presence of the LORD, and by his fierce anger. For thus hath the LORD said, The whole land shall be desolate; yet will I not make a full end. (Jeremiah 4:23–27)

In Isaiah 45:18, God declared that he had not created the world a wasteland. A wasteland is what it had become, a result of the war with Lucifer. Over this mess, the Spirit of God moved. God spoke, and there was light, and God called the light day and the darkness night. God spoke, and waters gathered and dry land appeared. God spoke, and a sun gave light and warmth by day and a moon gave light by night. As the Spirit hovered over the earth and God spoke, a supremely beautiful garden emerged. God looked upon all he had made and said it was very good.[22]

You wonder if this was the way it really happened. People can claim all manner of weird things as true that cannot be proven right or wrong. This is not one of them. There is scientific data that proves that the earth could have been created in six days. The catch is that unless you're trained in chemistry and chemical physics, you won't be able to understand the science. Scientists such as Dr. Edward A. Boudreaux have shown how everything could have happened in five days with man being created on the sixth day.[23] His data and formulas have been reviewed by his colleagues and found accurate. While the idea of a creator creating in six days brings into question many beliefs and teachings of numerous scientific disciplines, given that proof exists, logic requires us to admit that possibility.

Already, some traditional teachings are beginning to crumble. The

1980 Mount St. Helen's volcanic eruption has shown us that many of our geological beliefs are wrong.[24] That volcanic eruption did in a few hours and days what geologists once thought took millions of years. Scientific beliefs and theories are based on what we know up to now; they're supposed to change as more is known. All too often, theories are given the force of law without corroborative evidence.

The Garden, Satan, and the Fall

On the sixth day, God created a man and a woman in his image and likeness. They bore a resemblance to God in appearance and intelligence.[25] They were created a little less than the angels.[26] The glory that covered God covered them as clothing. God said to the man,

> I give you this planet earth to be its supreme rulers, to govern all the cities and countries and nations and world systems that come to be. I give you this earth with all its vast resources to develop them fully and make all that can be made from them, even vessels to sail among the stars. To seal this agreement, I give you this 6,000-year lease.[27]

While this was happening, Satan was lurking in the darkness. He dared not get close enough to let his presence be known. He looked upon this passing of a lease with great interest. Satan was delighted with what he saw. He knew how to get his earth and his kingdom back. He would use God's laws against him. The law said that the instant the man yielded to temptation and rebelled, he would die and the earth would become the property of the tempter. Until the moment when death overtook the sinner, the sinner would be the slave of the tempter.[28] Legally, it would be the same as trading the farm and yourself for a bowl of soup.

Satan could almost taste victory. With Adam's race—his new slaves and allies in rebellion and sin—he could once again amass the forces he needed to defeat God. Satan knew exactly how to get Adam and Eve to rebel. He would coax them to take pride in their wisdom. God had planted a tree in the garden whose fruit gave the knowledge of good and evil. God told them not to eat of the fruit of that tree or they would die. Satan's plan was to convince them they wouldn't die. God was just saying that, he would tell them, so when they were ready, they could eat it and would become much wiser than they were. After all, ruling the earth and its future kingdoms would take a great deal of wisdom.

Satan knew he couldn't personally tempt them; they would reject him instantly. But they wouldn't reject one of the created animals of whom at least one had the gift of speech. The serpent, arrayed in all his beauty and being smarter than all the other animals, was Satan's choice as the one animal most susceptible to vanity and pride. Satan was right. The serpent turned out to be an excellent choice for Satan's wiles. Eve, unsuspecting, believing she was talking to a talking animal that was in her care, convinced herself to believe it a wise thing to eat the forbidden fruit. After all, wisdom to rule wisely was what she needed. Surely, God would want that. Adam seemed to agree with her reasoning for he stood by her, and he also ate.

In one fell swoop, Satan got his planet. Instantly, Adam lost everything: his kingship, his planet, and the glory that had clothed him. Instantly, Satan got everything except the glory. This is the sad story of how our human race began.

A war was fought in the heavens among heavenly beings. It didn't involve the race of humanity, which was enjoying a marvelous and exciting life in a paradise surrounded by loving animals. In one instant everything changed. Man found himself in the middle of a war. The war in the heavens that hadn't involved him had become an actual war to be fought here on earth, and humanity was a principal player in the war.

Adam and Eve's eyes were opened, and they realized the horror of what they had done. As their glory faded, they were overcome by the fear of God's wrath. They hid. They tried to cover themselves so God couldn't see them. But the force of God's voice forced them to reveal themselves. Adam and Eve waited, expecting God's fury to come down on them.

The fury didn't come. Instead, they experienced deep sadness as though God were weeping and a great love as from one whose heart was breaking for them. As they listened, God comforted them and told them he had a secret plan and that one day the evil would be undone. It was a word of comfort to give them hope. God gave no details. Satan upon learning that God had a secret plan became furious.

Because his corrupted mind could think only evil, and not good, Satan could not imagine what this plan might be. His goal from then on was to watch for any clue, and then immediately do everything he could to destroy God's plan. We know today what Satan didn't know. We know that God's plan was a costly plan; a plan God had established before the beginning of creation, before Satan himself was created.

God's plan can be summed up in one phrase: kinsman-redeemer. God himself in the form of his Son would be born of a woman. He would be fully man, be tempted like us, yet be without sin. When the birth of Jesus came with angelic messages and angels singing, Satan finally figured it out. This was God's secret plan. Of all the stupid things God could do, Satan thought, he is becoming a man. Satan's evil mind quickly decided that all he would have to do was kill Jesus, who was God, and God would finally be defeated. He pursued every means he could imagine to kill the baby Jesus. Failing to do that he persuaded the authorities to arrest Jesus and kill him.

Despite his wisdom, Satan didn't know that the death of one who was without sin would instantly redeem all who were slaves of sin, if they received the gift. If that death were at the hands of Satan, all Satan's slaves would be set free from sin's dominion and from the control of Satan, the master of sin.

The gift would be there waiting, but it had to be received, appropriated.[29] All who have ever lived and ever will live have been delivered from the hands of death if they accept their deliverance. The redeemed will not be judged or punished. Instead, they will begin enjoying the redeemed life the instant they repent and believe. That includes being given authority over Satan and all the power of the enemy.[30]

Satan discovered to his horror that the act he thought would cripple God and lead to God's defeat had led to his own defeat. His slaves over which he once had authority now had authority over him. He found himself in a life-and-death battle trying to keep the redeemed powerless by keeping them ignorant of their rights and privileges.

The Future Is Bright

The above narrative is based on the facts in the Bible. The story flies in the face of theories of humanity evolving from some primordial soup. It asks us to believe in things we cannot see, taste, touch, smell, or hear. If we are honest, we must admit that stories of evolution also ask us to believe in things we cannot see, taste, touch, smell, or hear.

The creation story expects us to believe that humanity is not evolving up but instead fell from its high place as God's image. Man's sinful nature and everything bad that happens is a direct result of that fall. At the same time, the creation story gives man a reason for living, a purpose, and a destination. Evolution gives us no reason for being, no purpose for our lives, and no hope for life after death. Only the creation story gives purpose and answers the longing of the human heart for meaning.

A bright future is foretold. We are already in the period of last days as the Bible calls them. The Bible tells us that history is moving quickly toward an end. In the first part of the ending events, all who have chosen to let the Redeemer redeem them will suddenly be snatched up to a place called heaven. Once the redeemed have left the earth, Satan will have the freedom to set up his armies around Jerusalem. He will sit upon his throne and begin to rule for three and a half years at most.

During this time and the three and a half years preceding it, Jesus, the Redeemer, will be exerting a massive effort to get as many people as he can to join the army of the redeemed. Once that is done, he will return to Jerusalem with his armies. His and Satan's armies will meet in a devastating battle that will leave Satan's armies decimated and the Redeemer's armies untouched. Satan will be put in prison.

The story doesn't end. There will be a 1,000-year period under the rule of the Redeemer, Jesus, while Satan is in prison. All those who were in the army of the redeemed, who came back with him, will step in and fill the positions of rulership formerly held by Satan's vast army of angels.

We are told that at the end of the 1,000 years, Satan will be loosed from prison. He will immediately go about recruiting an army made up of millions of people who will rush to his side. Then will come the final battle. Satan will be utterly defeated and sent to his doom. With him will go the last of the angels and the last of the humans who joined his rebellion. This final battle will give people one last opportunity to choose on whose side they will serve—God's or Satan's.

When the final battle is over, there is yet one final event that will answer all the questions about the fate of the innocent people who were killed without having an opportunity to be redeemed. This is the great white throne judgment. All who have ever lived will be brought back to stand before God and be judged by their deeds. All who continue to choose evil will join their leader, Satan, in the lake of fire and live in torment for eternity. The rest will join God and the Redeemer in a new heaven and a new earth. That is where the book ends.

NOTES

CHAPTER 2

The Creator

Imagine sitting in front of your computer minding your own business. Suddenly, zap! Something hits you, and you instantly shrink to a half-inch in height. It will look to you as though everything in your immediate world has suddenly grown to 136 times its normal size. The chair you're sitting was only sixteen inches off the floor while you were about sixty-eight inches high. The distance to the floor is thirty-two times your height, the equivalent of 184 feet—a long way to jump.

What do you do? How do you let anyone know you need help? No one can hear you shout. You're too little to force a key down to leave a message on your computer. Besides, it will be a climb of 159 feet up to the keyboard. You must admit finding a solution looks hopeless. Let's hope the effects of the shrinking ray wear off soon.

What does this have to do with the incredible story in the previous chapter? We are facing a similar dilemma. Proving that the story is true seems just as impossible as you finding a way to get help when you are only a half-inch high. Yet the Bible expects us to believe that the story is true! We are to believe that creation was deliberate and that our primal ancestors were an extremely intelligent couple who fell into sin. We didn't evolve from some primordial soup but actually fell from our high place as godlike beings: "God created man in his own image, in the image of God created he him" (Genesis 1:27).

The usual ways of getting out of a mess don't work when you're only a half-inch tall. The usual ways of studying don't work either when you try to prove that the Bible is true. We'll have to figure out a different way to study. We want facts, empirical evidence we can get our hands on. We want to see the proof, but finding it is our problem. The Bible keeps insisting there is proof, but where is it? In all fairness, we should at least listen to what it has to say. To help us work our way through the Bible's story, we'll divide it into topics. The topic we will explore in this chapter is the Creator.

Beginning at the Beginning!

The Bible insists that there is a Creator who designed and created our vast universe. It insists there is a Creator, and it describes the Creator's personality, character, and even what he looks like. That's a lot of insisting! Don't say it's a preposterous idea just yet; we want to be fair to the Bible. Perhaps we can do that best if we approach it as though we have just awakened to life, just come to life in this world. We're seeing it for the first time. Our minds are open and searching for answers.

We ask, who are we? Why are we here? In answer to these questions, we're given a book we've never seen before. It is called the manufacturer's handbook, the Bible. This is the first we've heard of it, and for that reason, we know nothing of what is in it. We are told that it tells how everything came to exist. Naturally, we expect statements such as that to be backed up by proof. We want to avoid non-verifiable things such as opinions, beliefs, or philosophy. Logic will avoid those pitfalls and will best serve our purpose.

Logic is a way of examining what we can observe by using our five senses. For example, when describing a rose, we would record what our five senses told us. We wouldn't substitute a long discussion of why we like or dislike roses, or dwell on the philosophy of roses, or reflect on tales we've heard about roses. We would simply describe the rose—size, color, shape, form, structure, and fragrance.

In order to be logical, logic needs a starting point, something called an axiom. If you studied plane geometry in school, you may remember that it uses a set of statements that it calls axioms. An axiom is a self-evident truth, a universally accepted principle or rule. It cannot be proven; it just is. Though it is unprovable, there is a peculiarity about an axiom. The peculiarity is that while you cannot prove it's correct, you can prove it's not correct.

When you try to apply it, if it doesn't work, it's incorrect. That's the scientific method. You formulate an axiom and conduct experiments based on the axiom. If the experiments don't work, you conclude your axiom was wrong and formulate a new one. If the experiments work and provide the expected results, that "proves" for the time being that your axiom is true.

With that in mind, let us begin exploring the Bible with two axioms we cannot prove are true. The first is that there is a Creator, and the second is that the Bible is the Creator's revelation about himself. We'll begin by exploring the idea there is a Supreme Being, a creator God, as these are the first words of the Bible. It states it as fact. It makes no effort and evidently sees no need to explain it or justify it. This is our starting axiom: there is a Supreme Being with the aliases of God, Jehovah, and I Am That I Am.[1] Our challenge is to design an experiment to test the truth of that axiom. We search in our sourcebook, the Bible, for an answer.

The first thing we discover is that it tells us we have it all wrong! We think we're looking for a laboratory in which we can conduct experiments to test our axiom. The Bible says we are already in the lab and the tests have already been run! We are at the point that we need to record our observations and then draw logical conclusions. Our instructions on how to do this are detailed in the source book.

We ask, what were the experiments? What were the results? The Bible tells us to look at creation and record what we see. We can make some logical conclusions. The apostle Paul, author of thirteen books of the Bible wrote to the Christians in Rome insisting we could deduce the nature of God from the world in which we live.[2] Experts tell us that artists leave telltale marks on their artistic works by which experts can identify the author of a piece of art. "That," says Paul, "is what I'm trying to tell you!"

> For ever since the creation of the world His invisible nature and attributes, that is, His eternal power and divinity, have been made intelligible and clearly

discernible in and through the things that have been made (His handiworks). (Romans 1:20 AMP)

Many other places in the Bible teach that nature declares the nature of God. We are meant to understand this literally, not metaphorically. "The heavens declare the glory of God; and the firmament sheweth his handywork" (Psalm 91:1). Further, we are told that God's love for all humanity is plain to see in that "He maketh his sun to rise on the evil and on the good, and sendeth rain on the just and on the unjust" (Matthew 5:45). Logic tells us that if these statements are true, the declaration the heavens are making should be very clear and easy to understand. This brings us to the question, what is the handiwork the firmament is showing us?

Law and Order

Look at the complexity, orderliness, dependability, and reliability of the universe. Two words describe it: *law* and *order*. This is not the law and order of a political, legal system in which laws are passed and enforced. We're speaking here about what scientists have learned about how everything in our physical world works. Scientists call these law and order. Wherever we travel around our universe, the one characteristic shared in common by the largest planet, the smallest living organism, and the minutest part of an atom is what science calls law and order.

Everything that exists begins with the building blocks of the subatomic parts of the atom. These parts all relate to each other in a very specific, unchanging way. We call this orderliness law and order. Every configuration of these parts always produces the same results for each configuration. Law and order always determines what the whole becomes. Each configuration of electrons, neutrons, protons, and all the stuff in the nuclei of atoms yields its identifiable element. One configuration produces gold, another produces silver, and so on without exception.

The vast intricacies of scientific law and order are far too complex to suggest it happened by chance. Be logical, we are told. The laws of probability, the study of things happening by pure chance put the chance of the above happening by chance as one in a number so high we don't have mathematical concepts capable of expressing that number. The most logical conclusion we can make is that the universe with its law and order was a deliberate creation by an incomprehensible intelligence. In an effort to find some other explanation for the origin of the universe as well as the origin of humanity, numerous creation theories have been suggested. When followed to their logical conclusions, each of these theories has proven to be defective.

The big bang theory has risen to the top as the most popular in science. According to this theory, the universe came into existence roughly fifteen to twenty billion years ago. No theory as to the origin of the bang, or how it came about, is given. It supposedly began with an infinitely small and dense mass that exploded and expanded as it went. We're told that all the scientific laws came into existence in that same instance by chance. The alternative theory, intelligent design, requires acknowledging that there was a Designer/Creator, the God of the Bible: "In the beginning God created the heavens and the earth."[3]

Because the big bang theory appears to be the most logical explanation put forth so far, its flaws and holes are overlooked. One problem is that it doesn't take into account the immense speed at which the infinitely dense mass began to spread out or how it slowed down in an extremely short time, about three days.[4] Other problems with the big bang theory you don't hear about have to do with the rate by which the universe is expanding. As an example, consider the relative distance between the planets, their moons and suns, and their effect on each other.

Scientists have measured how much of our sun is consumed in a year. They have measured how far the moon and sun move away from the earth in a year. By calculating these figures in reverse, moving backward in time, they can estimate at what point in the past it was first possible for the earth to sustain life. As we move backward in time, the mass of the sun grows larger and its distance from the earth grows smaller. We quickly arrive at a time when the heat and effect of sunspots make life unsustainable, burning everything to a crisp. Likewise, as we move back in time, the distance between the earth and the moon grows smaller. A point is reached that the magnetic pull of the moon on the ocean tides and on all water sources is so great that life couldn't be sustained if there was any water that hadn't evaporated due to the sun's intense heat.

This means that the inhabitable earth is much younger than scientists first thought. Einstein discovered this when he formulated his general theory of relativity. In 1929, Edwin Hubble showed that distant galaxies were speeding away from the earth at an ever-increasing speed. Reversing these calculations, they could estimate backward to a time when the universe began and thus estimate how old the universe was. What they didn't calculate is the immense speed at which matter would have initially shot out from the big bang. It also means that using the scientists' own calculations, it is only in the last few thousand years that the earth could have sustained life as we know it.

The fascinating thing about this theory is that it comes close to fitting the pattern of how the Bible says God did it. The big difference is that the Bible removes the concept of chance, which is illogical, and in its place, puts deliberate act. You may not be comfortable with logic's conclusion that there had to be a Designer/Creator behind law and order. The thought of what that might mean disturbs some people, but law and order forces us to draw that conclusion. Logically, we must conclude that for law and order to exist, there had to be a Creator/Designer because the possibility of it happening by chance is utterly illogical and astronomically impossible, according to the laws of probability.

The Bible quotes God saying forcefully that chance had nothing to do with it.

> Where wast thou when I laid the foundations of the earth?
> Declare, if thou hast understanding. Who hath laid the
> measures thereof, if thou knowest? or who hath stretched
> the line upon it? Whereupon are the foundations thereof
> fastened? or who laid the corner stone thereof; When
> the morning stars sang together, and all the sons of God
> shouted for joy? Or who shut up the sea with doors, when
> it brake forth, as if it had issued out of the womb? When I
> made the cloud the garment thereof, and thick darkness
> a swaddlingband for it, And brake up for it my decreed
> place, and set bars and doors, And said, Hitherto shalt
> thou come, but no further: and here shall thy proud
> waves be stayed? (Job 38:4–11)

Look around you, the Bible tells us, and you will learn about the Creator. The majesty and grandeur of the heavens, the dependable cycle of the seasons with springtime and harvest, the wondrous beauty and splendor of nature, and the diversity of plant and animal life are things we can observe. Science has pushed back the boundaries of what cannot be seen by the human eye so we can picture the parts of the atom and understand a little about how atoms interrelate and act with each other.

God Is Good

Logic also tells us a creation governed by and existing by virtue of law and order requires a master designer whose nature is good. The reason his nature has to be good lies in the definition of evil. By definition, evil is the opposite of good and thereby opposed to law and order; they are mutually exclusive. Evil can produce only chaos, not law and order. Evil cancels law and order because by definition they are opposites. They cannot coexist; coexistence would be illogical.

Conversely, law and order cannot produce evil. Law and order can produce only good; this is a universal and fundamental law. Think of it this way: you have two buckets of paint. One is white and the other is black. They cannot coexist in the same bucket; the instant you introduce the tiniest amount of black into the pure white, it will never again be pure white. Once the white is contaminated by the black, it can never do the task it was designed to do. Jesus talked about this when He stated,

> For there is no good (healthy) tree that bears decayed (worthless, stale) fruit, nor on the other hand does a decayed (worthless, sickly) tree bear good fruit. For each tree is known and identified by its own fruit; for figs are not gathered from thorn bushes, nor is a cluster of grapes picked from a bramble bush. (Luke 6:43–44 AMP).

If the goodness from which law and order proceeds was to have the tiniest bit of evil or chaos in it, it would cause intermittent failures in the things law and order do. Gravity keeps us from flying off the earth. If it failed due to the impurity of evil and chaos, we'd go flying off into space and die instantly. There can be only one or the other. Remember, our approach is logic.

Logic tells us that when you add +1 and -1 you get zero. You can have one or the other, not both. Because the universe embodies law and order, we logically conclude the designer must by nature be good. We also conclude that logically, his will for his creation must also be good inasmuch as evil by logical definition is opposed to and at war with him in whom no evil can exist. James put it this way.

> Every good gift and every perfect (free, large, full) gift is from above; it comes down from the Father of all that gives light, in the shining of Whom there can be no variation rising or setting or shadow cast by His turning as in an eclipse. (James 1:17 AMP)

Man-Made Gods Are Worthless

It would be illogical not to recognize the majesty, glory, sovereignty, and the invisible attributes of this designer God. This may not be the conclusion one wants to reach, but what other conclusion is there if we stick to logic? Logic is the principle Paul and the psalmists pushed. Logic is based on observable facts; anything else would be unsustainable opinion. "And the heavens [as the visible universe, the sky, atmosphere, etc.] shall declare his righteousness: for God is judge himself" (Psalm 50:6 AMP). "The heavens declare his righteousness, and all the people see his glory" (Psalm 97:6).

This is the point where something illogical happens. A loud NO, heard and unheard, is voiced by those who reject any suggestion that there is a creator God. The above facts are rejected outright. Logic is rejected. Some people want nothing to do with the concept or possibility of a creator God whose nature is good and whose will toward them is good. Paul didn't say why they rejected the possibility of a creator God; he just said they did. Paul wrote that men should have been thanking and glorifying God for what was plainly visible. Those who refused to be awed by the observable universe were without excuse.

> So men are without excuse, altogether without any defense or justification, Because when they knew and recognized Him as God, they did not honor and glorify Him as God or give Him thanks. But instead they became futile and godless in their thinking with vain imaginings, foolish reasoning, and stupid speculations and their senseless minds were darkened. Claiming to be wise, they became fools professing to be smart, they made simpletons of themselves. (Romans 1:20b–22 AMP)

They didn't just refuse to be awed; they abandoned all logic and denied the existence of God. They were not content to leave it at that; they seemed compelled to make up their own gods and religions fashioned after their selfish designs and vain imaginings. They didn't want to give reverence and honor to the God pictured by creation itself and so easily revealed by logic. "And by them the glory and majesty and excellence of the immortal God were exchanged for and represented by images, resembling mortal man and birds and beasts and reptiles" (Romans 1:23 AMP).

The Bible affirms that the Creator continually watches over his creation. His will towards it is good and not evil. Therefore to him honor and glory are due. Instead of just ignoring God's existence, the men who refuse to acknowledge God create idols to replace him. Is there a logical explanation for that behavior? The only one that makes sense is rebellion, like thumbing your nose at God.

Man, having rebelled and rejected the Creator, designed his own gods and deities. The motivation for designer gods was to have a god man controls who in turn controls things over which man apparently has no control. Some deities have to do with different aspects of life such as good harvests. The elders of each tribe faced with needing to control public behavior and control crime often used witchdoctors and taboos (control by fear).

In crisis situations, man-made gods always fail. People who turn to God and seek his help only in desperation create an awkward situation for themselves. They've denied his existence for so long that they've blinded themselves to who he is or what he is like as revealed in the natural world.

Logically, if the God to whom we appeal is powerful enough to help us, we can't be his designer; he can't be a fairy tale we make up. A genie-in-a-bottle type of God won't work. It is only logical that if we were powerful enough to create the Creator, we wouldn't need him because we would be the creator!

So we must conclude that there is no way we can logically have the kind of God we need on the one hand and on the other hand be his boss, master, and creator as is the case with all man-made gods. The logical, rational, conclusion is that if this God exists, if this creator of you and me has created us for a purpose, if there is any purpose behind our existence, this God must reveal himself to us and tell us why he created us and explain the destiny that awaits us. Does such a revelation exist?

NOTES

CHAPTER 3

Pilot Torture

Learning to fly a Piper Cub was easy. Well, almost easy. A Cub is a simple plane. My ground-school training before I took my first flying lesson was simple stuff I already knew. It covered the controls and how to use them and takeoff and landing speeds. Preflight inspection meant checking the controls, looking for oil leaks or broken safety wires on bolts, looking for holes in the fabric, and checking the gas (there were no gas stations in the sky).

After only eight hours of practice using the controls in actual flight, the student is ready to solo. I found that takeoffs and landings weren't hard as long as I didn't oversteer and start zigzagging back and forth on the runway. The hard part came after being airborne. I had to bank the plane in the direction I wanted to turn while applying just the right amount of rudder and a little up-elevator. I didn't do it right at first, and the plane started doing funny, bobbing, up-and-down things. So did my stomach.

My experience in that small simple Piper Cub was a far cry from the experience of a man I know who learned to pilot a twin-engine jet. He was given thick manufacturer's manuals to study. He was expected to study them and to know the jet inside and out, rivet by rivet. His actual flight instruction took place inside a flight simulator that duplicated the cockpit of a jet with all the controls, lights, and instruments, and the view outside the windows of the cockpit.

In the simulator, the student finds himself sitting on the tarmac, and is expected to do everything by the book. He receives clearance from the tower to start the engines, taxi to the runway, and prepare to take off, and finally take off. The simulator simulates every detail. Once airborne, the student flies to his destination following all the protocols for a safe landing, pulling up to his designated parking area, and shutting down the engines.

Once he has mastered those simple procedures the student discovers in a nerve-racking way just how important those manuals are. He steps inside the simulator expecting another normal practice flight, but it turns out to be anything but normal. Suddenly, everything that could go wrong goes wrong. He's in the middle of a nightmare! He has an engine on fire, all his electrical fails, he's got a hydraulic leak, the weather's bad, and his wings are icing up. What does he do? He crashes and dies. The door of the simulator opens, and he steps out shaken to the core by what just happened.

The student pores over the manufacturer's manuals. He reviews everything that happened and tries to find the answers to what he should have done. Then he goes back into the simulator only to have it happen again and again. One pilot said, "I know what this is. It's pilot torture!"

When flying a jet, if something goes wrong, the pilot can't park the aircraft and call Triple A. We are thankful that pilots undergo this rigorous training so they know how to respond in every situation that might arise including their worst nightmares. Learning what to do to save his life and the lives of everyone on board is why studying the manufacturer's handbook and trusting the wisdom of its writers is an absolute must for a jet pilot.

The Jet's Handbook Meets Form Criticism

Let's examine the jet plane manufacturer's handbook in the same way textual experts examine the Bible. First, we note that the manufacturer, presumably the company CEO, claims to be the author of the book. Second, the manufacturer claims that the book is without error.

Our textual experts tell us immediately that the manufacturer couldn't have written it. Their initial cursory examination shows that it was written by many people. There are a variety of writing styles. It was written over a long period time, and some of the authors died before the book was published. Closer examination shows that the manuals are a collection of the accumulated knowledge and wisdom of many people gained from developing, testing, and flying the jet.

Despite the fact that many people wrote the manufacturer's handbook, the authority of the handbook is not diminished. The need to study and know the handbook backward and forward is an indisputable requirement for pilots in order to safely fly the jet. Textual criticism and literary analysis of the manual doesn't invalidate the information in it.

The application of the same literary analysis to analyze the jet plane manual as is used on the Bible helps us understand certain key facts. First, as with the jet manuals, the variety of authors and expanse of time doesn't invalidate or alter the integrity, reality, and truth of the Bible. Second, just as the jet manual originates from and are the intellectual property of the manufacturer, so too is the Bible, God's Word, his property. There is one difference, however. When you buy a jet, you want to know about the manufacturer and his integrity. You might even visit the factory to watch the plane being built. But you can't do that with the Bible, which claims God created us and that the Bible is our manufacturer's handbook. How do we check God out?

Logic has led us to conclude that there is a God, a Supreme Being who created this immense universe. This Creator created designer cells and genes for every living thing and all the elements and determined the exact number of mitochondria each living cell needed to fulfill its designed function. We also concluded that this being would by definition be far above our ability to communicate with or comprehend. That is our dilemma; we want to see our manufacturer face to face, find out what he is like, and learn if we can trust him.

In a sense, we want to personalize the Creator, give him a human face. Logic told us some things about him by observing his handiworks. This enabled us to deduce some aspects of his character. Logic also made us realize that unless he reveals himself to us, we will never get to know him. This forces us to ask, Has God revealed himself to us in some other way we've missed? If he has, where do we find that information? If that information exists, we would logically expect the source of that revelation to be flawless and undeniably true.

The Enigma of the Bible

When we look for this revelation, what do we find? All we find is a Bible that claims it is God's revelation. This is not good news; it seems to put us on shaky ground. The Bible appears to be one of the most flawed, unreliable, and most unlikely sources of accurate knowledge. In the face of all that, the Bible has the audacity to say, "Trust me!" That is illogical.

Now what do we do? The only thing we can do at that point is to be fair and logical. We're going to proceed on the assumption that the Bible is exactly what it claims to be: God's revelation about himself and us. This was not a problem in the case of our jet manufacturer's manual. The fact that it has many authors and was written over a long time doesn't bother us because we can prove its validity by repeating the development of the jet, and we can visit the manufacturer and watch the jet being built. We can't do that with the Bible. That forces us to adopt our second axiom mentioned earlier—the Bible is the Creator's revelation about himself and us.

The Bible appears to be divided into sections according to the type of writing. It begins with history. Mixed in with the history are pages and pages of rules and regulations called laws. There's even a section on medicine. There is poetry and advice called proverbs. Quite a large section is called prophecy. It ends with more history and letters. It is obvious that the Bible comes from the pens of many authors who wrote over a long time. We see the personalities and imprint of the men who wrote it just as we did with the jet's manuals.

All our information about the Creation, Lucifer's rebellion, what happened to man, and the subsequent history of the Jewish nation along with most of the prophecies telling what will happen in the future are in the Old Testament. Examples are Genesis 1–3, Isaiah 14:12–17, Ezekiel 28:13–17, and Daniel 12. When we look at this variety obviously written by many authors as was the jet manual, it is hard to think of it all coming from one source. But if we keep in mind that the jet manufacturer's handbook came from one source but had many authors, it isn't so hard to believe.

From the beginning, we find God saying to individuals, "I am God, and there is none else." Conversations with God began with Adam and Eve and continued after they were expelled from the Garden of Eden. These conversations continued through Moses and the prophets. There was never any question in the minds of the hearers as to who was talking. In the context of all this diversity, the Old Testament stands its ground and states that the whole thing is God's words, that God's words are settled in heaven, and that they are true. It tells us that what God has said he would do he will do. It says that God magnifies his word above all his name: "I will not leave thee, until I have done that which I have spoken to thee of" (Genesis 28:15b). "Every Word of God is pure" (Proverbs 30:5). "So shall my word be that goeth forth out of my mouth: it shall not return unto me void, but it shall accomplish that which I please, and it shall prosper in the thing whereto I sent it" (Isaiah 55:11). "For thou hast magnified thy word above all thy name" (Psalm 119:89, 160, 138:2).

Laws of Probability

Probability is the likelihood of some event occurring or of two of more events occurring at the same time. For example, if you put five different-colored marbles in a sack, what is the probability of putting your hand in the sack and pulling out the red marble? One in five. What's the probability of five people reaching into the sack and each pulling out the red marble? Much higher.

Interestingly, the Bible has the laws of probability on its side to support its claims. The Old Testament contains more than 300 references to a coming Messiah, Jesus. The Old Testament, the first half of the Bible, was written by people who lived between 400 to 1,500 years before the birth of Jesus. During that period, many of the writers talked about the coming of the Messiah and made over 300 prophecies about his coming and his mission. One might be tempted to ask, so what? That is until one realizes that the New Testament claims that Jesus the Messiah fulfilled those 300-plus prophecies!

What is the probability of that happening? The laws of probability tell us that the chance for just 8 of these prophecies to be fulfilled in one person would be 1 in 10 followed by 16 zeros. For 48 to be fulfilled in one person would be 1 in 10 followed by 157 zeros. What do you suppose the probably would be for one person to fulfill all 300-plus prophecies? We cannot begin to imagine that number.

With respect to these prophecies, Jesus quoted the Old Testament: "The scriptures cannot be broken."[1] He said his purpose in coming was to complete the Old Testament.

> You must not think that I have come to abolish the Law or the Prophets; I have not come to abolish them but to complete them. Indeed, I assure you that, while Heaven and earth last, the Law will not lose a single dot or comma until its purpose is complete. (Matthew 5:17–18 Z PHP).

The laws of probability apply to the statements of the jet manufacturer as well as to Jesus. The difference is that no one doubts the statements about the jet and its performance as written in the jet manufacturer's manual. The manufacturer will tell you that you'd better believe every word in the handbook or die. The fact that it has many authors has nothing to do with its authority. Everything is there to keep the plane flying and you alive.

The Bible's message is the same. Believe every word in the handbook or die. Both books will tell you everything is there for your benefit. It's just that it is so much easier to believe that about a machine than it is to believe it about a person. We are helped in our struggle to deal with this by the words Peter spoke for all the disciples when he said that Jesus was the Son of the Living God.[2] They had firsthand experience and found it all to be true just as the handbook had said. This is the message they proclaimed from the temple mount to the farthest cities declaring that God was

> Personally present in Christ, reconciling and restoring the world to favor with Himself, not counting up and holding against men their trespasses but cancelling them,

and committing to us the message of reconciliation (of the restoration to favor). (2 Corinthians 5:19 AMP)

Bible Critics Are Illogical

This brief examination of the Bible shows that it has no problem seeing itself as God's revelation about himself, which is our second axiom. It views itself as being the repository of our knowledge about the creator God and insists that the breath of God is in all that is written. In making these bold claims, the Bible has laid itself wide open to being blown out of the water if anything shows up to prove any of its claims are false.

While we cannot prove the Bible is true, we need to ask, has anyone proved it's not true? That is a critically important question. Remember, we are being guided by logic—has anyone come up with any concrete evidence rather than mere opinion?

When we examine the evidence presented by the many who have claimed to have disproved the Bible, no one has yet disproved any of its content. Instead, we discover a very interesting tactic used by so-called scholars and other experts who desire to prove the Bible false. They switch their tactics from presenting concrete and empirical proof that the content is wrong, which they are unable to do, to using innuendo. Without actually saying it, their intent is to discredit the Bible by various scholarly means. These scholars bombard us with dissertations about form criticism, comparative religions, folklore, and myth.

By analyzing style (form), and what are considered irregularities, some scholars have concluded that the Pentateuch (the first five books of the Bible) is actually a blending of four literary strands labeled J, E, P, and D. This has led some to conclude that an editor had taken parts of myths from other cultures such as the Gilgamesh epic[3] and woven them together to form what we now call the Pentateuch, or Five Books of Moses. The book of Isaiah, they insist, is actually three books written by three authors and therefore couldn't have been dictated by God. The belief seems to be that if you can discredit the authorship of the Bible, you can discredit the truth it proclaims. Can you imagine so-called experts trying to do that to the jet's handbook? We'd laugh at them.

The purpose here is not to review all the articles debunking the Old

Testament, New Testament, and life of Jesus; there are ample examples of these on the Internet. As illustrated by comments by Bill Maher[4] and broadcasts about the evolution of the earth and man by *NOVA* on PBS, these debunking efforts center around arguing that there is no archeological evidence to support the Old or New Testament accounts. Programs such as *NOVA* and writers focused on debunking the claims of the Bible purposely choose as their experts and sources of reference only those with whom they agree.

Archeology Says It Really Happened

One of the favorite places for attempting to debunk the Old Testament has been the story of Moses and the miracle of dividing the waters of the Reed (Red) Sea.[5] We will spend some time with this because it was a fascinating, dramatic, key event in Israel's history that illustrates the difficulty in obtaining accurate data.

There has been much controversy about the crossing because it's a mind-boggling concept. We're talking about a substantial body of water splitting in two while about two million people and their cattle cross on the dry seabed. Then the walls of water come back together and drown Pharaoh's sizable army.

We must admit that this event as described in the Bible is not easily believed. But just because something isn't easily believed doesn't mean it didn't happen. In this case, those trying to debunk it have been forced to rely on flawed information and assumptions. First in the list of evidence they present is the lack of any mention of the Hebrews in Egyptian writings.

Unfortunately, political realities seriously hamper archeological research today. Concerning the lack of written records, two things need to be said. First, no pharaoh or king wanted to be remembered for his defeats; he would have seen to it that those events were expunged from the records. Because of its religious makeup and enmity with Israel, Egypt today is not friendly to the idea that a Jew, Joseph, was a ruler of Egypt or that two million people under Moses had caused a series of plagues and then fled from Egypt destroying Pharaoh's army in the process.

Archeological research by non-Egyptians is almost impossible.

Records from other cultures have indicated that there was a sizable group of people who came out of Egypt invading and capturing as they went, but it doesn't identify them.

Second in the list of evidence debunkers present is their conclusion that there was no body of water to be parted. Trying to make a logical story that deviates from the biblical narrative leads to problems. The explanations offered to explain the Red Sea crossing raise more problems than they solve. This popular version arbitrarily shortens the number of days the Hebrews traveled from twenty to three before coming to the sea.

Tracing a three-day journey on their maps, they assumed it had to be the present-day Red Sea. They claim that the water was shallow where Moses crossed and that winds blowing across the marshes at that point often left the rocky seabed exposed. They conclude that the idea that God divided the waters is a myth. They offer no explanation as to what happened to Pharaoh's army, which evidently drowned in three inches of water.

The Bible tells a different story. Four hundred years had passed since Jacob and his children had settled in Goshen. They had grown in number to about two million. A new pharaoh came to power who turned the Israelites into slaves. They cried out to God, and God sent Moses to demand that Pharaoh let the people go. Pharaoh refused to give up his slave labor. Each time Pharaoh refused, a plague was sent on Egypt but not on the Israelites in Goshen. The last plague was the death angel that passed over and left unharmed all the Israelites but killed the firstborn of the Egyptians and the firstborn of their cattle. The grieving Pharaoh and the grieving Egyptians demanded that the Israelites leave and loaded them down with the wealth of Egypt.

The Israelites fled. To follow their path, we need to reconstruct the geographical setting as it was around the fifteenth century BCE as shown by archaeological evidence. The East Nile River at the time of the crossing was sixty or seventy miles to the east of its present location where it flowed through the ancient city of Ramses. There was no Suez Canal. The water level in the Gulf of Aqaba and the Gulf of Suez was several feet higher with the two gulfs extending farther north.

In the area just east of today's Suez Canal were several large freshwater lakes connected by canals. These lakes, called reed lakes because of the reeds surrounding them, protected Egypt's eastern border. The international trade route from Egypt to Canaan, called the Horus Way, crossed a bridge at the north end of the northernmost lake, Ballah Lake. The bridge was fortified with additional fortifications to the east.

God told Moses not to go to Canaan by the Horus Way. They would have to fight, and the people were not ready to fight. Instead, they followed a route God designed for them. God explained that this path, along which he was leading them, would make Pharaoh think they were trapped with no escape. Pharaoh took the bait. He came with 600 chosen chariots and all the other chariots of Egypt to capture the two million Hebrew slaves who were cornered. They overtook the Israelites where they were encamped by the Reed (Red) Sea. God held Pharaoh's army back with a cover of darkness while a wind divided the water and dried the freshwater seabed. Israel crossed on dry ground. The cover of darkness lifted, and Pharaoh's pursuing army attempted to cross the seabed in their chariots. The chariots got bogged down in mud. Once the whole of Pharaoh's army was on the seabed, the waters came back together and drowned the soldiers. There was not a single survivor.

The Bible is very precise in its detailed description of the location of the crossing: "before Pihahiroth, between Migdol and the Reed (Red) Sea, before Baalzephon."[6] These places no longer exist today, and for a long time, their locations were unknown. However, they did exist at the time the account was written. It is illogical that the Bible would pinpoint the exact location of the crossing if the story were myth.

That being the case, the question is, what happened to the cities? Blame the pharaohs! The ancient pharaohs wanted a canal where today's Suez Canal is. Many attempts were made to dig it by hand. During all this digging, they ended up draining the fresh water lakes. The desert immediately took over. The people left. It is logical to assume that the people who had lived in those cities as well as wandering Bedouins scavenged what they could from the cities and lakebeds; sand and desert winds hid the rest.

Today, there is nothing visible that matches the story. However, recent archeological, geological, and textual evidence has been showing up enabling archeologists to tentatively locate boundaries of the fresh water lakes, the connecting canals, and the location of several cities. To date, their findings show that the crossing point had to be the middle of Ballah Lake, just south of the Horus Way Bridge. The only way across would have been to divide the water.

There is a second competing theory that places the crossing point at the Gulf of Aqaba. While convincingly presented with videos, charts, and claims of artifacts on the gulf floor, this theory has been challenged as a scam. Those who argue against this theory do it on the basis of the originator's lack of academic credentials, failure to follow accepted scientific methods, etc. Regardless of whether this location, or the first, or a different one is the location of the crossing, the Bible insists on a specific location where the only way across would be if the waters did in fact divide.

Many people do not want it proven that the event actually happened. They do not want to deal with the possibility that Israel's God exists. In our quest to be led by logic, we cannot be one of them. We have to go with logic and conclude that the preponderance of available evidence says it must have happened. On this point, the Bible challenges us again.

Built-In Guarantees

The Bible says it is accurate and that it has built-in guarantees of its accuracy. Paul told Timothy, "All Scripture is God-breathed and is useful for teaching, rebuking, correcting and training in righteousness" (2 Timothy 3:16). Peter also said,

> Above all, you must understand that no prophecy of Scripture came about by the prophet's own interpretation. For prophecy never had its origin in the will of man, but men spoke from God as they were carried along by the Holy Spirit. (2 Peter 1:21–21)

Jesus told His disciples that the Bible had its own Guarantor whose job it was to help them remember exactly what He had taught them.

> But the Comforter, which is the Holy Spirit, whom the Father will send in my name, he shall teach you all things,

and bring all things to your remembrance, whatsoever I have said unto you ...Howbeit when he, the Spirit of truth, is come, he will guide you into all truth: for he shall not speak of himself; but whatsoever he shall hear, that shall he speak: and he shall show you things to come. (John 14:26, 16:13–15)

According to Jeremiah 1:12, God guaranteed His Word: "I will watch over my word to perform it." If God personally guaranteed his Word, the Bible, does that apply to his promises as well? He made some rather bold statements concerning power to do miracles and authority over evil forces that he gave to those who had faith in him.

Everyone wants power. Years ago, there was a television series called *Bewitched*. It was the story a beautiful witch, Samantha, who fell in love with a mortal, Darrin. Samantha could do anything she wanted by simply twitching her nose—set a fancy table with gourmet food, clean house, etc. All of us at times have wished we had that kind of twitchy nose power to take care of unpleasant chores. The amazing thing the Bible teaches is that we do have power, not the twitchy nose kind, but power even more amazing. Jesus told his disciples, "I will do whatever you ask in my name, so that the Son may bring glory to the Father. You may ask me for anything in my name, and I will do it" (John 14:13–14 NIV). That statement is almost unbelievable, not the sort of thing science teaches us. But Jesus kept insisting it was so. He said,

These signs will follow those who do believe: they will drive out evil spirits in my name; they will speak with new tongues; they will pick up snakes, and if they drink any poison it will do them no harm; they will lay their hands upon the sick and they will recover. (Mark 16:17–18 PHP)

Many claim that none of these scripture promises is worth the paper it's written on. If true, that would mean God isn't watching over his Word to perform it. Others say they've tried the promises and they didn't work. This of course would invalidate the Bible's claim. However, others have looked at the promises and discovered there are conditions attached to each promise. Their unanimous testimony is that if one meets the conditions, the promise works. They have filled volumes with their testimonies often giving irrefutable proof.

This concept of first meeting the conditions is something many people don't want to hear. It's like me telling my mom I want her to bake me a wild strawberry shortcake and Mom hands me a basket and says, "Go pick the berries and hull them and then I'll bake it." That wasn't what I wanted to hear. I wanted her to do everything. Instead, she actually expected me to do something first. That's how God's promises work. Do the man side first, and God will do the God side. People are often not aware that there is a man side to every promise. This lack of knowledge as well as an unwillingness to do the man side has been a major source of trouble.

What can we conclude with respect to our second axiom, the Bible's claim that it is the Creator's revelation about himself and us? All God's promises have been demonstrated to be true. In spite of all the scholars' attempts and in spite of all their opinions, conclusions, and reputations, no one has been able to prove any of the Bible's claims to be false. Logic dictates that we must therefore conclude that the Bible is what it claims to be.

People can refuse to believe the Bible, make fun of it, scoff at it, or suggest that those who believe it are idiots, but that doesn't disprove it. That's merely expressing individual attitudes toward it. The reputation of the writer doesn't change the truth. Fire still burns whether a notorious crook or a renowned scientist tells us it does.

NOTES

CHAPTER 4

Wizards and Sorcerers

Long ago in the days of King Arthur, England's legendary hero, it was said that there was a wizard named Merlin, a confidant of King Arthur who possessed much secret knowledge as well as the ability to prophesy the future. It was also said that the spells and magic for which he was famous were all written in his books and could be taught to an apprentice. That was a time in history when superstition ruled because science was lacking.

Merlin was a legendary figure, a mixture derived from bits of fact mixed with legend. There probably was someone named Merlin about whom tales were told much in the manner in which rumors grow in the telling. Some writers pictured him as a ruthless, evil man, and others pictured him as a saint depending on the story they were telling. I prefer to think of him as the wise and lovable old man who tutored the future King Arthur in Walt Disney's movie *The Sword and the Stone.*

In the days when people believed in such things as wizards who possessed these powers, everybody who was anybody wanted his own wizard. That was especially true of kings such as the legendary Arthur. To have a wizard of Merlin's rumored reputation among his advisors would put the fear of god into any king's enemies. Of course, wizards like that didn't exist, but hey, it didn't do any harm to let your enemies think you had a powerful wizard on your side.

God Is Not a Legendary Character

Don't confuse the legends of the Middle Ages when superstition reigned with the story the Bible is telling. There is no legend, no mixing of bits of stories to make one good story in the Bible. Even though in some men's minds God might appear to function like a legendary wizard or sorcerer, his character doesn't derive from them. Rather, wizards and sorcerers derive their character from man's wishful thinking mixed with historical events such as Moses parting the Red Sea and striking a rock to release water.

Merlin's character was changed to fit whatever role the storyteller wanted him to play. That does not and cannot happen with the God of the Bible; it is a logical impossibility. What is true of Jesus, God's Son, is true of God concerning whom Paul wrote,

> Jesus Christ (the Messiah) is (always) the same, yesterday, today, (yes) and forever (to the ages)" (Hebrews 13:8 AMP).

> God said, "For I am the LORD, I change not" (Malachi 3:6).

> The psalmist wrote, "Before the mountains were brought forth, or ever thou hadst formed the earth and the world, even from everlasting to everlasting, thou art God" (Psalm 90:2).

When we consider our universe, logic leads us to conclude that not only is there a creator but there absolutely must be a creator; there is no other logical explanation that fits the facts. Logic at this point has us over a barrel. If we argue that the biblical story of Creation is a compilation of many creation stories, we still must answer the question of how it occurred.

As we have seen, the probability of it happening by chance is illogical. The only logical conclusion is that the creation was a deliberate act by an intelligent power that could speak things into existence. That brings us back to the Bible, which says, "In the beginning God (prepared, formed, fashioned, and) created the heavens and the earth" (Genesis 1:1 AMP).

The Bible emerges unscathed by attempts to prove it isn't God's story about himself and about how he created the universe.

God Is a Person

Now we can ask the question of all questions: where did God come from? We won't get an answer. The Bible doesn't tell us where God came from. It does say that God is from everlasting to everlasting. It says he never changes. But it does give us an idea of what God looks like and what he is like as a person. These attributes are an important part of the Bible's story. They are also important to us in as much as the Bible says that man was created in God's image and likeness.

Man was originally designed to have one-on-one fellowship with God; that fact is reassuring. Though the fellowship was lost because of man's rebellion, that knowledge gives us confidence that God knows and understands us. That confidence applies to the question, what does God look like?

While the Bible assures us that God does not look like man, it does tell us man carries a vague and flawed resemblance to God. According to the Hebrew in which the Old Testament was written, man was created in the image (*tselem* in Hebrew) and likeness (*demooth* in Hebrew) of God.[1] The word *tselem* has the meaning of shadowing forth. The word *demooth* has the idea of model, pattern, appearance. Man, as first created before the Fall, was a representation of God modeled and patterned in appearance and intelligence like God.

Physical similarities between man and God are pointed out many times in scripture. God's right hand is exalted and doeth valiantly.[2] Moses, facing obliteration in the presence of God's face, is protected by God's hand that allows him to see only God's back.[3] Jesus said, "He that hath seen me hath seen the Father" (John 14:9). The godlike brilliance of the mind man once possessed is suggested by Genesis 11:6 (AMP) in which God said, "And now nothing they have imagined they can do will be impossible for them."

God Is Power

As important as it is to know that God is a person, the question that is of far greater importance is, what kind of a person? We know he is a creator and therefore possesses ultimate power. Think about all the wizards and sorcerers dreamed up by authors and projected onto the screen by special effects. Some are pretty spectacular. Surrounding each one in the various authors' minds is the idea that there is tremendous power emanating from the sorcerer, power that crackles with sparks flying. You don't want to touch the sorcerer or stand too close to him when he is in the midst of his sorcery. You instinctively sense that he could as easily disintegrate you as to look at you or even turn you into a frog!

Nowhere in the Bible is it suggested that God turns people into frogs. However, these stories of sorcerers and wizards suggest that there is an aspect to God's being that people tend to overlook—his unimaginable power. Raise the power of our fictional sorcerer a few notches. What would his appearance be like then? Would we see sparks flying out from him if not flashes of lightning and rolls of thunder? Might he even glow? We always picture the person who possesses that kind of power as emitting those kinds of outward, physical signs. A common man may possess a weapon, but the sorcerer is the weapon!

In the movie *Howard the Duck*,[4] an alien overlord temporally inhabits the body of a physics professor. The alien, using the professor's body, goes on a search for energy. His eyes glow, and powerful lightning shoots from his eyes blasting cars and people out of his way. That is not what God is like, but it does give a tiny glimpse of the wonder and power that had to be emanating from our creator God during creation. He has the power to merely speak their names and the planets and stars filled the vastness of nothingness creating space as they did. That much power is beyond our imagination.

What would it be like to have the intelligence to design everything and know how it would fit together from hydrogen atoms, to the most complex piece of electronic engineering, to spaceships sailing the galaxy, and merely speak the word and have it instantly come into being? To have that kind of knowledge, to have the power to simply speak a thing into being is beyond our understanding.

God Is Holy

We come back to our original question, what is God like as a person? We already know he is something we are not—holy. Understanding the meaning of holiness as it applies to God is critical. Holiness describes God's character as "totally good and entirely without evil."[5] Logically, that means nothing can exist in God's presence that is not 100 percent compatible with his holy nature.

Envision God as the ultimate sorcerer who is altogether holy. The power that emanates from him is holy because he is holy. His holiness acts like a refiner's fine. All dross, all impurities will be annihilated in the presence of his holiness. An ice cube melts in the presence of heat not because the heat is willfully directing its heat toward the ice cube but because an ice cube cannot exist in the presence of heat.

In like manner, what does not conform to God's holiness cannot exist on its own. It cannot have a separate life apart from his holiness. If it did, it would be a logical impossibility. Remember that +1 plus -1 = 0.

Another way to look at holiness is to see it as meaning to be perfectly conformed to the original design and thus to be a perfect fit and therefore usable. When I worked on airplane engines, safety was the ultimate concern when it came to every repair. Any bolt, nut, gasket, washer—any part that didn't conform to the original design and therefore didn't fit perfectly—was "unholy" to the engine. Only that which was holy, which conformed to the original design and was a perfect fit and which worked perfectly was allowed to become part of the engine. My boss used to remind me that I would be the first person to fly in the plane when we took it up for a test flight. Was I willing to fly with the repairs I'd made and the parts I'd used? I naturally threw away any "unholy" parts.

Pump that illustration up a few notches to God-sized. When it comes to God and the awesome power emanating from him, it doesn't take much imagination to realize that anything that isn't holy, anything that doesn't conform to his nature will instantly cease to exist in the presence of his power. It will be consumed like dross, annihilated. It is logical that that will happen.

When Holiness Doesn't Work

The fact that holiness must annihilate dross is of critical importance and yet it doesn't. Why? The answer has to do with the heart and soul of the Bible's message. To get to that, we must deal with the apparent failure of holiness to do its job. It is obvious that not all that is unholy has been consumed and annihilated. If the unholy gets annihilated in the presence of God's holiness, why does unholiness exist? Why is there sin, war, cruelty, suffering, and evil? Has God wandered off someplace where dross is beyond the reach of his holiness?

We need an answer because a bunch of things are going on that shouldn't be happening if God is holy and cares about us. There was the war in heaven with Satan still on the loose. There's Adam and Eve, who continued to live despite their rebellion. And there is the fact that you and I are alive! What does logic have to say about all this? The answer of course is simple; at least, logic would suggest a simple answer. Realistically, it is the only answer it can suggest. Some kind of force field, to borrow a term from science fiction, must be shielding us from his holiness, his consuming fire (Hebrews 12:29). If that is true, we must conclude that God is shielding his creatures from his holiness for some purpose.

Before we consider God's purpose, we need to look at God's wrath and anger. What happens when the unholy comes in contact with God's holiness? It experiences God's wrath. If you were refining gold, you would heat the gold so hot that all the dross, the impurities that float up to the top, would be burned off. From the impurities' point of view, the fire they are experiencing is the anger and wrath of the hot gold. Gold is inanimate. No brains. No emotions. People are animate and have emotions. Our emotions run the gamut from love and joy to anger and wrath. We assume that God must also share that gamut of emotions since we were created in his image. Does he?

My father was a gentle man. His love for me was never in doubt. But I did discover at an early age that he had an anger and wrath side. At times, I caused wrath and anger to arise in him. Even though he controlled his anger, he was determined to burn off all my dross. He had an old-fashioned leather razor strop he used to sharpen his straight razor.

He also used it to "sharpen" me. Boy did that thing sting! I tried sticking a dustpan in my pants to absorb the blows. Doing so was a mistake. He was not amused.

His spankings were not cruel, and the pain I felt was more from the fact that my dad had spanked me. Spanking me didn't make my dad happy either; he didn't want to spank me even though I had it coming. It was something he felt he had to do for my own good. He believed in Proverbs 19:18: "Chasten thy son while there is hope." After a spanking, when I went to bed that night, dad would always come and sit by me, almost apologizing for spanking me, and tell me he loved me. Keep that thought in mind. God does not take pleasure in subjecting people to his anger and wrath, but when it's necessary, he always does it in love.

Imagine that the gold spoken of above is by nature and not by any outside assistance always so hot that impurities are instantly burned up when they come into its presence. The impurities experience the heat from the gold as the gold's anger and wrath. God's holiness is like that; it is so great that nothing unholy can exist in its presence. Because it's being burned up when it comes into the presence of God, the unholy describes the "spanking" it is experiencing as God's anger and wrath.

The Hebrew words translated as "glory" and "goodness" link the holiness of God to the mystery of his power and to his character as totally good and entirely without evil. God told Moses that his glory was his goodness.[6] Holiness includes goodness, graciousness, mercy, and lovingkindness. Logically, that is what we would expect God to be—the opposite of evil and chaos. These characteristics are basic requirements to be a law and order creator.

This is where my imagination runs wild again. In the movie *Raiders of the Lost Ark*,[7] it was rumored that the box or ark that had rested in the Holy of Holies of the temple in Jerusalem had been found. It was further rumored that the ark contained the rod of Aaron, a piece of manna (the food eaten by the Hebrews in the desert), and the two stone tablets on which were inscribed by God's finger the Ten Commandments. Supposedly, these items possessed a tremendous source of raw energy. It was believed that whoever harnessed this power could rule the world.

It was a race to see who would find the ark first and in so doing possess its power. In the movie, the evil men got to it first. When the evil men opened the ark, they came face to face with God's holiness experienced as wrath. They melted away—a gruesome but effective depiction of what happens when evil comes into the presence of a holy God unshielded from his awesome holiness. Wrath is how evil experiences holiness. God is an all-consuming fire.[8]

In the encounter of Moses with God on Mount Sinai in the desert of Midian, God told Moses,

> Thou canst not see my face: for there shall no man see me, and live ... I will cover thee with my hand while I pass by: And I will take away mine hand, and thou shalt see my back parts: but my face shall not be seen (Exodus 33:20–23)

The Force Field of God

This brings us back to the idea of a force shield protecting us. God protects us from exposure to his holiness. That helps explain why Satan is still around. Satan is under God's protection because God is using Satan, the traitor, to help him achieve his purposes. Because God asserts that he is from everlasting to everlasting,[9] meaning he has no beginning or end and is unchanging, logic leads us to conclude God had a purpose, a goal, a design, a destiny in his work of creation and will achieve it. Whatever it turns out to be, logic tells us, it involves man because man was not destroyed.

Before we leave the subject of God's holiness experienced as wrath and anger, let's look at an example of it in action. But first a warning. Don't attribute human emotions to God; that's a common mistake that causes confusion. God warned us, "'My thoughts are not your thoughts, neither are your ways my ways,' saith the LORD. 'For as the heavens are higher than the earth, so are my ways higher than your ways, and my thoughts than your thoughts'" (Isaiah 55:8–9).

God's anger and wrath are not emotions that get stirred up. Our anger and wrath are emotions; they well up in us. Sometimes, we let them rule us to the point that we lose control. It is a logical impossibility for God to be ruled by anger and wrath as we know them; they are negative and opposed to the holiness, love, and joy that logic requires of a creator God. The story of Noah and the flood is a good illustration of the God kind of wrath and anger. We will see in a surprise ending to the story that God's love and desire for our best is central to his anger and wrath.

Looking at the flood from a human point of view, it looks as if God had become very angry and had blown his stack when he flooded the earth. Let's examine the story.

> And GOD saw that the wickedness of man was great in the earth, and that every imagination of the thoughts of his heart was only evil continually. And it repented the LORD that he had made man on the earth, and it grieved him at his heart. And the LORD said, I will destroy man whom I have created from the face of the earth; both man, and beast, and the creeping thing, and the fowls of the air; for it repenteth me that I have made them. (Genesis 6:5–7)

The word *repent* as it applies to God in the Bible is always different from *repent* as it applies to man. Man repents in remorse because he is in trouble and turns from sin to God. When God's actions suggest that he changed his mind or was doing something else, the Hebrew also labels it as repent. That is how it appears to us. However, the Bible assures us that God and his purposes are unchanging. If God doesn't change, logically, that leaves us with just one thing that does change—man's conduct. By his conduct, man moves himself from judgment to grace or from grace to judgment. If man refuses to repent, a judgment of his own making comes upon him because sinning has caused him to move outside God's protective force field.

If we step out from under the protection of an umbrella in a rainstorm, we'll get wet, repent of that, and step back under the umbrella. The Bible says God repented and sent the flood. What actually happened? Some who are intrigued by the mythical story of Atlantis believe the flood was an event man brought upon himself. It's said that a great calamity caused Atlantis to sink into the ocean and all life to be lost some 12,000 years ago.

Inasmuch as nothing is heard about Atlantis until 360 BC, when Plato told the story in his *Timaeus*, its existence can be only speculation.

What interests us is that one possible reason given for its destruction was that the Atlantians were experimenting with some source of crystalline power. It got out of hand, and they blew up their world. Imagine for a moment that the story of Atlantis is actually a retelling of the story of the flood that details what had happened. The Bible tells us, "The wickedness of man was great in the earth, and that every imagination of the thoughts of his heart was only evil continually" (Genesis 6:5). Evil seems always to lead to a self-induced destruction.

In most cases, Hebrew cannot be translated directly into English. Translators were limited by their level of knowledge at the time the Hebrew was first translated into English. There has been a tremendous growth in knowledge since then. When the Bible was first translated, the Hebrew word *rawkeeah* was translated as "firmament" Genesis 1:2 tells us, "And God made the firmament, and divided the waters which were under the firmament from the waters which were above the firmament: and it was so." Now we know that the word translated firmament, *rawkeeah*, means beat out as in a transparent metallic overlay. Analysis of this word and its use has led some scientists to believe that it means that in the beginning, a transparent metallic overlay like a shield existed high above the earth. The overlay was a metallic form of hydrogen. Metallic hydrogen has been produced in the laboratory and can exist high in the atmosphere. There is no reason why it couldn't have existed at creation.

If there was a transparent, metallic, hydrogen overlay, what was its purpose? Scientists have speculated that its purpose was to be part of the earth's ecological system. It shielded the earth from harmful solar radiation. According to the Bible, prior to the flood, rain was unknown. Instead, the earth was watered by a mist that rose up from the ground.[10] In conjunction with this is fossil evidence showing that the oxygen level of the earth at the time of the flood was over twice what it is now.

This has led many to theorize as to what might have happened. Like the legendary Atlantians, was it possible that sinful man was doing something that was threatening to disrupt the earth and cause the breakdown of the hydrogen canopy? We are told that anything man can imagine, he can do.[11] We aren't given any ideas as to what advances in science or technology man may have made up to that time. Did man himself cause the flood? All we know for sure is that God was not taking a whip and beating up on man in anger; that would have been contrary to his holiness. He wasn't stomping on the ground and going off and pouting.

What did cause Noah's flood? There is geological evidence that the world underwent a dramatic geological and climatic change about that time. Could something have caused the hydrogen canopy to break down and combine with the oxygen in the air as seems suggested in the story of Atlantis? Could man have caused volcanic eruptions? For the first time in earth's history, it rained and it kept on raining. The breakdown of a hydrogen canopy that combined with oxygen gives us a logical source for all the water and explains why it took forty days to empty the skies.

What is clear is that at that point, God's response to what unrepentant, sinful man was doing to himself was to let it happen. If man will not repent, if man resists every offer of grace God offers him, then God will repent of protecting man from himself. When the umbrella of God's protection is removed, man experiences God's holiness as anger and wrath. In a very real sense, man self-destructs.

All the people except for Noah and his family perished. Was this the story of a vengeful and wrathful God destroying all he had made like a potter destroying a vase that didn't turn out right? No! "As I live, saith the Lord GOD, I have no pleasure in the death of the wicked; but that the wicked turn from his way and live" (Ezekiel 33:11).

A Loving God Is a Fair God

God did not annihilate the people as though they had never lived; he loved them still. The only way he could love them still is that while their physical bodies were in the ground, their spirits, the real people, were still alive. No details are given concerning this in the Bible, but Jesus did say,

> And as for the matter of the resurrection of the dead, haven't you ever read what was said to you by God himself, 'I am the God of Abraham, the God of Isaac and

the God of Jacob'? God is not God of the dead but of living
men! (Matthew 22:31–32 PHP)

People whose physical bodies perish are still alive in a place God has
set aside. We don't know where it is or what it is like, but this fact brings
us to the surprise ending mentioned above. Can you guess who the first
people were to whom Jesus went after his resurrection, the first people
to hear the good news? It was to the people who had died in the flood.

He [Jesus] went and preached to the spirits in prison, The
souls of those who long before in the days of Noah had
been disobedient, when God's patience waited during
the building of the ark in which a few people, actually
eight in number, were saved through water. (1 Peter
3:19–20 AMP)

Sometimes, logic cannot give us all the answers. When discussing *agape*
love, the kind of love God has for man, we come across one of those times.
Let me explain it this way. Water is composed of two atoms of hydrogen
and one of oxygen. Whenever you combine those two elements in that
ratio, you'll get water. If you use electrolysis to separate the elements in
water, you will always end up with two parts of hydrogen to one of oxygen.
Love, by comparison, is not something you can analyze in a laboratory. For
this reason, it does not fit in with our theme of law and order.

The only way we can use logic when speaking about agape love is to
first define what is meant and develop a list of actions by which we can
judge if agape is present in any given action. The same is true with other
attributes of God such as defined by John, who said God was light,[12] and
by Paul, who said God dwelled "in the light which no man can approach
unto" (1 Timothy 6:16).

The reason this is a concern for us is that these are all qualities we
consider a part of holiness, a part of what we expect God to be as we
experience him from the safety and protection of his umbrella, his force
field. When the rebellious person, the unholy person, steps out from
under the force field, he is directly exposed to God's holiness that he then
experiences as God's wrath and anger.

NOTES

CHAPTER 5

Outsmarted

My high school science teacher encouraged us to ask questions and experiment on our own to see if we could find the answers. The good and the bad about experimenting is that it involves free will. You have to make some choices, decide what you will and will not do, decide how to do it, and hope you haven't made bad choices. Some experiments ended up as science exhibits. Others were disasters.

Explosions

My friend and I experimented with hydrogen gas, which burns with a blue flame. We figured out a way to produce hydrogen. Our test to see if we had actually produced hydrogen was to ignite the gas. If it burned with a blue flame, we would know we'd been successful. Because water is the by-product of burning hydrogen, we decided to conduct our experiment over a pan of water.

We inverted a glass funnel over the experiment to collect the hydrogen gas and funnel it to the small end of the funnel. Once we had pure hydrogen was coming out of the funnel, we would ignite it. This is the point at which we began to question our choices. A bit unsure of the results, we put a match on the end of a yardstick, ducked under the lab table, and lit the hydrogen. The explosion sent pieces of glass, water, and equipment flying all over the place. Our teacher, who had been watching and knew we would be safe, just sat at his desk laughing. It took a lot longer to clean up the mess than to conduct the experiment, which of course didn't end up as a science exhibit.

The encouragement to ask questions and design experiments spurred me on. My mind would travel in many directions asking, why not? One direction had to do with a story I read about a scientist traveling back in time to when the earth was young and life was just beginning to appear. He tried to be very careful as he walked about and examined this prehistoric world, but he accidently stepped on a plant and killed it. When he returned to our present time, he discovered he had done irreparable damage. The world he once knew had changed dramatically. For example, the letter *e* had disappeared from the alphabet! It was just a story, but it raised an intriguing question in my mind.

The story made it clear that time travel for going into the past or the future to interact with events thus actually changing history or the future was not a good idea. In fact, it could end up creating utter chaos, a logical impossibility in a universe of law and order.

My youthful science experiments and the story of the scientist who changed history raised questions in my mind about the Bible's story of prehistory and man's subsequent creation and fall. A discordant note was sounded that shouldn't have been allowed in a creation founded on law and order. To see what I mean, we will go back to the absolute beginning.

A Luciferian Explosion

Most of what we will witness was described in chapter 1, so we'll skip over most of that. Hopping into a time machine, we will go back and pick up the story where Lucifer, the guardian of God's glory, is described. We'll witness Lucifer's fall into sin and darkness.

> You were the signet of perfection, full of wisdom and perfect in beauty. You were in Eden, the garden of God; every precious stone was your covering, sardius, topaz, and diamond, beryl, onyx, and jasper, sapphire, emerald, and carbuncle; and crafted in gold were your settings and your engravings. On the day that you were created they

were prepared. You were an anointed guardian cherub. I placed you; you were on the holy mountain of God; in the midst of the stones of fire you walked. You were blameless in your ways from the day you were created, till unrighteousness was found in you. In the abundance of your trade you were filled with violence in your midst, and you sinned; so I cast you as a profane thing from the mountain of God, and I destroyed you, O guardian cherub, from the midst of the stones of fire. Your heart was proud because of your beauty; you corrupted your wisdom for the sake of your splendor. (Ezekiel 28:12–17 ESV)

Exactly what he did was written in another place.

How you are fallen from heaven, O Day Star, son of Dawn! How you are cut down to the ground, you who laid the nations low! You said in your heart, 'I will ascend to heaven; above the stars of God I will set my throne on high; I will sit on the mount of assembly in the far reaches of the north; I will ascend above the heights of the clouds; I will make myself like the Most High. (Isaiah 14:12–14 ESV)

We watch these events in dismay. It's difficult to understand how one so beautifully adorned and entrusted with so great an honor could fall into evil when evil by its very nature cannot exist. We watch bewildered as he falls into sin and becomes Satan. We watch him persuade and influence a third of the angels to join him (Hebrews 12:22). With this army and his belief in his superiority, he launches an attack on the throne of God. That goes against law and order.

And there was war in heaven: Michael and his angels fought against the dragon [Satan]; and the dragon fought and his angels, and prevailed not; neither was their place found any more in heaven. And the great dragon was cast

out, that old serpent, called the Devil, and Satan, which
deceiveth the whole world: he was cast out into the earth,
and his angels were cast out with him. (Revelation 12:7–9)

We are grateful that when the smoke clears, Satan is defeated, not
God. With Satan's ranting and raving echoing in our ears, we bring our
thoughts and our time machine back to the present. Much as when a
movie ends, we step into the foyer. We smell popcorn, smile, and think,
It was only a movie.

But this time, there is no smell of popcorn. We are haunted by what
we saw and the questions it raised in our minds. Did it actually happen?
Why did Lucifer rebel if he had been created perfect? If the story is true,
why wasn't Lucifer obliterated when he turned evil? It doesn't make
sense, and it makes the Bible's story hard to believe. Besides, what we
saw happened before man came on the scene. So it doesn't really affect
us. Does it?

The Gift of Dominion

The story does affect us because what enabled Lucifer to rebel was also
given to Adam and Eve—they had the freedom to obey or rebel. This
was not what many call free will. The concept of free will does not exist
in the Bible. Decision making, however, was automatically part of the
assignment God gave to Adam and Eve when he told them,

> Be fruitful, multiply, and fill the earth, and subdue it
> (using all its vast resources in the service of God and
> man); and have dominion over the fish of the sea, the
> birds of the air, and over every living creature that moves
> upon the earth. (Genesis 1:28 AMP)

God was saying, "You do the work. You make the decisions. This is
your place and your responsibility now." This explanation does not answer
our questions. Since all creation must adhere to law and order, how
could something God created that was perfect turn evil? Having turned
evil, how could it continue to exist in the presence of God's holiness in

violation of law and order? If the biblical account is true, there should be logical answers. Logic tells us that if iniquity was found in Lucifer and it hadn't been there in the beginning, then iniquity was something Lucifer had the ability and authority to take upon himself. This was not free will as free will is usually interpreted. Lucifer and Adam received the freedom to choose to love and trust and obey God or rebel.

The word *rebellion* as used here doesn't mean unrest, resistance, and chafing under a cruel regime that generates rebellion in our day; it means the result of choosing to rely on one's own wisdom and judgment rather than God's. Ezekiel tells us that Lucifer chose iniquity: "Your heart was proud because of your beauty; you corrupted your wisdom for the sake of your splendor" (Ezekiel 28:17 ESV).

From references such as this, it's easy to infer that when God created the angels, he designed them to be rational, thinking, intelligent, living, immortal beings. God created the angels with the capability of making independent intelligent decisions; as was true for all conscious creatures. This is a logical conclusion based on the fact that that is what they did! "Are not the angels all ministering spirits (servants) sent out in the service (of God for the assistance) of those who are to inherit salvation?" (Hebrews 1:14 AMP).

Free Will Isn't Free

This ability to make independent, intelligent decisions often called free will is generally defined as the ability to make choices free of restraints. However, there is no such thing as freedom from restraints. As one of my professors used to say, "Your rights end where the other person's nose begins." The moment I invade your nose, I am in deep trouble!

There are always restraints. I can decide which clothes I'll wear to work, but if I decide not to wear any, I'll discover all manner of forces arrayed against me. Apparently, the exercise of my free will is conditional on the free will of many others. Against my free will, they will not allow me to be naked at work! Against my will, they will clothe me and lock me up! Evidently, I wasn't free to will what I wanted to will.

Aside from such trivial things as what clothes to wear, I have the free will to make choices that shape my life, that determine what happens to me and what kind of future I will have. I can choose to be governed by my emotions, or by reason, or by my faith. I can choose to be the victim of whatever circumstances or situations befall me, or I can choose to rise above them and create new circumstances for myself.

Though I want to proclaim I am the captain of my soul, a self-made man, all my choices are always made in the context of things over which I have no control. I can choose to be an actor, but I cannot choose which parts I'll be offered. I cannot control how much audiences will like me. I can choose whom I want for friends, but I cannot force them to be my friends.

Logic forces us to conclude that free will is nothing more than the freedom to choose between two or more possibilities. Opposed to this is the fate of the robot, which is forced to follow a predetermined path. This is not the same as the gift God gave of being able to choose to love him or rebel (disobey him). Logic forces us to conclude that free will is nothing more than the freedom to choose between two or more possibilities but we can't make the possibilities. Logic forces us to conclude that it is of great importance to God that all who choose him have done so because they want to, not because they are forced to.

The Bible gives a fairly clear explanation as to why we have been given this freedom. It is God's desire that we come to him of our own free choice.[1] He does not force us to love him, serve him, or accept his gift of forgiveness and redemption. He wants us to come freely because we want to come.[2]

Punishment Delayed for a Season

Perhaps now we can answer the question why Lucifer and we weren't annihilated when iniquity was found in us. If as logic dictates God couldn't create evil and that evil cannot exist in his presence, how do we account for the fact that none of the rebellious malefactors were annihilated? Why has Satan been left free to interfere with everything God does?

Logic gives us two choices. One is that Satan was too powerful for God. That choice does not compute. The thing created cannot be more powerful than the one who created it. The other choice is that God has intervened and delayed the punishment. Rebellion carries within itself its own punishment, just as a red-hot stove will burn your finger if you touch it. While God cannot stop the punishment, he can will it to be delayed so that he can use the rebellious ones to help him accomplish his ultimate will.

This conclusion is supported by the Bible. We are told that corrupted angels were doomed to live forever in the lake of fire that was prepared for the devil and his angels.[3] At the final judgment, all who have joined Satan will also be doomed to spend eternity in Satan's lake of fire.[4]

Satan: Even His Evil Serves God's Will

One example of how God uses Satan to accomplish his ultimate will is told in the story of Joseph and his brothers.[5] The fact that God had an ultimate plan was hinted at in the Garden of Eden after man's rebellion. "I will put enmity between thee and the woman, and between thy seed and her seed" (Genesis 3:15).

We first become aware of the details of God's purpose and plan when God asked Abram to leave his family and travel to a land he had never seen. Attached to this call was a promise.

> And I will make of thee a great nation, and I will bless thee, and make thy name great; and thou shalt be a blessing: And I will bless them that bless thee, and curse him that curseth thee: and in thee shall all families of the earth be blessed. (Genesis 12:2–3)

Up to that point, all Satan knew was that God had a plan that was not going to be good for him and his plan to defeat God. When God announced that in Abraham all the families of the earth would be blessed, Satan knew God was starting to unfold his plan.[6] The details of Satan's failed attempts to stop the plan are recorded in Genesis. God repeated his promise to Abraham to Abraham's son, Isaac, and to Isaac's son, Jacob. Up to that point, Jacob's family was just a family. It was now time to grow this family into a nation.

God needed to put them in a place where they could prosper and grow in numbers in safety. The land of Goshen in Egypt was the best agricultural land around. That was where God chose to settle his man Jacob so the nation could grow. How did he do it? He used Satan! It began with Jacob's sons and their jealousy of their brother Joseph.[7] Satan had listened in on all God's conversations with Abraham, Isaac, and Jacob. He knew that God's next step would be through one of Jacob's sons. But which one?

When Joseph told his dreams to his brothers and father, saying they would be bowing down to him, Satan knew Joseph was the key. Get rid of Joseph and stop God was Satan's plan. Joseph's brothers were already furious with Joseph's dream telling. Satan fed their anger and tried to get them to kill Joseph.

What Satan didn't know was that God had planned for Satan to stir up the brothers' hatred. Neither did Satan know that God had arranged for a caravan to be passing by. Satan, realizing he couldn't get the brothers to kill Joseph, put it in their heads to sell Joseph into slavery thereby getting rid of him forever. The brothers did that and explained to their father that Joseph had been eaten by a wild animal.[8]

Step one of God's plan to use Satan to accomplish his will was done. God knew how Joseph would respond. Joseph, a slave, from that time on conducted himself as accountable to God. The result was that God's favor was upon him. He was sold to Potiphar, who saw how everything Joseph put his hand to was blessed. He made Joseph his head servant. But being the head servant in Potiphar's house was not the place where God needed him to be. Satan was not happy with where Joseph was either. In all likelihood, Potiphar had been thinking of giving Joseph his freedom.

So, Satan used one of his demons of lust to get Potiphar's wife to lust after Joseph. Joseph refused her advances. Potiphar's wife was steamed. Also, scared. She feared that if Joseph told Potiphar what had happened, she would be in big trouble. So, she lied to Potiphar before Joseph could say anything. Potiphar had no choice but to throw Joseph in prison.[9] Satan was enjoying this because it meant Joseph would be hidden away in prison and be the slave of prisoners for the rest of his life. Satan had done it. God was defeated.

But not so. Prison was where God needed Joseph to be to finish his training and to be in the right place at the right time. It was in prison that Pharaoh's chief butler would become aware of Joseph and learn that

Joseph could interpret dreams. A day came when Pharaoh dreamed a dream that no one could interpret. The chief butler remembering his time in prison told Pharaoh that Joseph could interpret dreams.

Pharaoh sent for Joseph, and upon hearing the interpretation of his dream and seeing the wisdom of Joseph's suggestions as to what to do, he elevated Joseph from the lowest of the low to second only to Pharaoh in ruling Egypt. That was where God needed Joseph to be for the final phase of His plan.[10]

Satan was furious about how God had used him and tried to kill Jacob and his family by a severe famine (In Ephesians 2:2 Paul writes that Satan is the prince of the power of the air). He absolutely didn't want them to grow into a nation. God had other plans and used the famine as the means for getting Jacob to send his other sons to Egypt. They thought they were going to buy food. When Joseph's brothers arrived in Egypt, they discovered much to their shame what had happened to Joseph. The guilt-ridden brothers feared for their lives while their families and Jacob rejoiced.

So it was that Joseph, with the needed blessing of Pharaoh, brought his father, Jacob, and all his brothers and their families to Goshen. There they settled and enjoyed nearly four hundred years of peace during which they grew into a nation. To his scared brothers, who had good reason to be scared, Joseph explained how all these events had taken place according to God's plans: "Ye thought evil against me; but God meant it unto good" (Genesis 50:20).

As Joseph's words illustrate God uses Satan's evil plans to accomplish his will. This leads us to conclude that God has temporarily blocked the consequences of sin in order to accomplish an ultimate good. Joseph's story was just the beginning. Other scriptures seem to support this conclusion.

We are faced with two realities. First, that God has suspended the punishment of evil to accomplish his purposes. Second, we are now faced with two kingdoms: the kingdom of light (God) and the kingdom of darkness (Satan). We are faced with the fact that there is no neutral ground, no secure hiding place where we are not the slaves or servants of the ruler of one kingdom or the other. God has given us the free will to choose between the kingdom of light or the kingdom of darkness. It is up to us to pick our kingdom.

> Know ye not, that to whom ye yield yourselves servants [slave, bondman] to obey, his servants [slave, one who gives himself up to another's will] ye are to whom ye obey; whether of sin unto death, or of obedience unto righteousness? (Romans 6:16 AMP)

NOTES

CHAPTER 6

From Disaster Springs a Family

When we reflect on the Bible's creation story with its enemy invasion, we must admit that it sounds incredulous. It is almost akin to reading a *Star Wars* saga with different characters but similar stories. In fact, it has everything in it to rival epic stories such as *Star Wars* and *Dune*. It begins with a God we cannot see, angels we cannot see, and then a master fallen angel and demons we cannot see. The bad guys are out to take over the world and then the universe using us as slaves.

All these events and participants would come to life and be visible in a cinematic production. As in *Star Wars* and *Dune*, we expect the good guys to win, but in our story, it doesn't seem they will unless something unforeseen happens. Some things make us question how powerful God really is.

Hurricanes, tornadoes, earthquakes, and weather out of control leave horrendous trails of destruction in their wakes. For some, everything that was important in their lives is wiped out. If you were one of those people, you'd be sick to your stomach. That's how we felt when our time machine left the scene of desolation following Satan's failed attack on the throne of God.

When we left the scene in chapter 5, the earth was a mess; it was covered in a black, smoky slime. We were in shock that a being created so perfect in every way, so beautifully adorned, would turn on his Creator to usurp his Creator's throne. If God is all powerful, why would he allow that to happen? Why does God allow natural disasters to happen?

Could it possibly be that God is not so all powerful after all? Cinematic productions like *Star Wars* and *Dune* show good winning over evil and always through the heroism of men who are empowered by the good. We don't see that happening here. The answer that God is not all powerful is not logical in light of what we have learned about God. Are we missing anything? Logic forces us to keep looking.

We are not disappointed! It seems that there is an ultimate purpose, an ultimate goal toward which things are moving. The Bible tells us that God has a plan he put in place long before our world was created, long before Satan came on the scene.[1] We are not told that it was inevitable Satan would rebel. We are only told he had the choice and made it of his own free will. God used Satan's rebellion to help accomplish his ultimate will. The good guys will be empowered to win after all! God is in control. His will for us is good. As the verse below states, it sounds as though God is planning to build a family, and we are part of it!

> According as he hath chosen us in him before the foundation of the world, that we should be holy and without blame before him in love: Having predestinated us unto the adoption of children by Jesus Christ to himself, according to the good pleasure of his will. (Ephesians 1:4–5)

Let's return to our time machine and go back to pick up the story just before God forms or reforms the earth. Using two Hebrew words, *tohoo* and *bohoo*, Genesis 1:2 tells us that the earth was a wasteland of emptiness and devastation. When these two words are used elsewhere in the Bible, it is always with this same meaning. We watch God through his Spirit move over the earth's chaos and make it a garden of delight (Eden).

We watch God place a man, Adam, and a woman, Eve in the garden. They are our grandparents many times removed. They are created in God's image and after his likeness. They bear a resemblance to God in appearance and intelligence. The glory that covers God covers them as clothing.

How might the conversation have gone between Adam and Eve and God? Perhaps God gently wakes up the man and woman he has just created. "Wake up, Adam and Eve, and see your kingdom. Look out from this garden, this temple in which you stand. As far as you can see and farther still is a world for you to love and rule. You, Eve, have been taken out of your husband's side to work together and help each other. I give you, Adam and Eve, the earth to be its supreme rulers, to govern all the cities, countries, nations, and world systems that will come to be. I give you this earth with all its vast resources to develop them fully and make all that can be made from them, even vessels to sail among the stars."

As we listen to God's instructions, we catch a movement out of the corner of our eyes. Someone or something is watching under cover of darkness. We are suddenly aware that Satan, the rebellious leader of the failed angelic rebellion, has been eavesdropping, watching what is happening, and listening to God's instructions to Adam and Eve. Suddenly, all the prehistory we had watched that we thought didn't involve us raises its ugly head to haunt us. The Garden of Eden is being invaded!

God speaks again. "To seal this agreement, I give you this 6,000-year lease." Satan's ears perk up. He wants the lease God has just given to Adam. It's quite possible that Satan mistakes the lease for a title deed like the one that had once been his. But this was only a lease, not a title deed. The earth belongs to God.[2] Unknown to Satan, there is a lot of fine print in the lease.

Satan is delighted by what he hears. It is almost as though his kingdom had been given back to him. Like mounds of frosting on a cake, not only will he get his kingdom back, it will also come with all the godlike, intelligent slave labor he can use! We see his evil mind at work as he devises a plan to trick this "God image" out of the lease. "Easy as pie," we hear him murmur. "Get the man to become proud of his own wisdom. If he becomes wise in his own eyes, it won't take much coaxing to get him to eat from the Tree of the Knowledge of Good and Evil."

Satan knows that the instant Adam rebels or disobeys God, Adam and his whole race yet unborn will automatically become the slaves of sin and subject to himself, the sin master.[3] The deed to the earth will automatically pass to him, Satan. That is the law. Now, how to do it? He can't personally talk to Adam and Eve; they wouldn't fall for it. But what if one of the animals did the talking? They'd never guess Satan was behind it. He picked the vain and proud serpent to be his lackey.

When did the temptation happen? Right then, or later? I think later. Satan has a massive ego; he considers himself superior to God. Taking candy from a defenseless baby was not his style. This makes me think Satan would have waited until Adam and Eve had a full grasp of their powers and abilities. His ego and pride would logically require that he deceive a fully mature Adam and Eve to prove he could outwit God and then rub God's nose in his failure. It's one thing to seduce a baby with a piece of candy but another to seduce a mature man with promises of more power.

What do you imagine Adam and Eve had achieved prior to the Fall? Not a single hint is given. They had been created in God's image and after his likeness. That means they must have also possessed massive intellects and a fair measure of God's knowledge as well as some of his power. If Satan delayed the temptation, isn't it possible they could have made many strides in technological development prior to the Fall?

Be that as it may, during the time leading up to the Fall, Adam and Eve were citizens of God's kingdom of light. As earth's monarchs, rulers of all they surveyed, they had the responsibility to rule the animals and develop this planet's resources. It's possible that all the animals had the gift of speech and that they talked with the animals. We know they talked with the serpent, who was the shrewdest and most crafty of the animals.

The serpent under Satan's coaching began to engage Eve in conversation about the Tree of the Knowledge of Good and Evil. He did it by suggesting things that weren't true. Eve, wanting to correct the serpent and trusting in her wisdom, went a bit too far and deceived herself into eating the forbidden fruit. Adam, who was with her, evidently agreed with the idea that more knowledge was good and ate the fruit as well.

That choice cost them their lease as well as their freedom. The word *lease* is not in the biblical account. However, there is evidence that there was a legally binding agreement between God and Adam. When Satan spoke to Jesus in Luke 4:5–7, he referred to this lease and the fact that he possessed it. Satan couldn't have possessed it if Adam hadn't had a legal right to surrender it to him. "The devil said unto him, All this power will

I give thee, and the glory of them: for that is delivered unto me; and to whomsoever I will I give it" (Luke 4:5).

With the lease went Adam and Eve. Their citizenship suddenly switched from the kingdom of light to the kingdom of darkness. The damage to the human race was far worse than merely switching kingdoms, worse than the fact that all Adam's descendants were also transferred to the kingdom of darkness as slaves. The damage was bad—human nature was changed, genetically altered. Adam's god-nature was changed into a sin-nature that has been passed down genetically to us all. "As it is written, there is none righteous, no, not one" (Romans 3:10). "But we are all as an unclean thing, and all our righteousnesses are as filthy rags" (Isaiah 64:6). "Wherefore, as by one man sin entered into the world, and death by sin; and so death passed upon all men, for that all have sinned" (Romans 5:12).

The fact that Adam had descendants raises a question. God had told them that if they ate that fruit, they would die.[4] They should have died instantly. "For the wages of sin is death" (Romans 6:23). "The soul that sinneth, it shall die" (Ezekiel 18:20). Adam and Eve were supposed to die. What happened? Instead of dying, they become the walking dead. Actual death was somehow temporarily suspended. They remained alive but in a different kingdom, changed from being masters to being mastered and fulfilling the mission Satan assigned them.

Well, actually, as Satan soon discovered, that was not exactly how it worked out. Remember the fine print in the lease? God had thrown a couple of wrenches into the machinery of Satan's plans. Satan knew nothing about it until he heard the *clunk*; his plans came to an abrupt halt. Satan had figured that since he was still alive, it meant God didn't have the power or authority to destroy him. That meant God couldn't legally destroy any of Satan's property either.

Adam and Eve were now Satan's property, a new part of his army of rebels. These new recruits, or slave labor, were much smarter than the stupid demons. Yes, things were looking much better now or so he thought until he heard that *clunk*. It meant Satan wasn't getting all the free labor he thought he was getting! Things went downhill for Satan right from the get-go. Ever since then, he has been fighting the humiliation of

God using his carefully planned evil to accomplish God's purposes as we saw in the story of Joseph.

Instead of the earth becoming the platform for his next attack on the throne of God, the earth itself has become the battlefield. Instead of being part of his army, Adam's race became his enemy. Frustrated at every turn, Satan has turned loose every evil in his arsenal in an effort to discourage man, to intimidate man, to tempt man in every way.

Don't make the mistake of thinking Satan has godlike powers to create or do anything. All he has is his voice; he is dependent on men listening to him and doing his evil for him. This is risky because he knows every believer In Christ has been given authority over him. He doesn't dare let man find out that God has given man the authority to stop him in his tracks.[5]

This brings us to the answer to our question, why does God allow disasters and suffering? There were titles of authority that came with the lease God had given Adam: prince of the power of the air; the god of this world; the prince of this world.[6] All nature was under Adam's control. Satan became the owner of these titles and the authority that went with them when he took control of the lease. As a result of the Fall, nature itself was thrown into confusion.[7] Satan's titles mean quite simply that Satan is in control of tornadoes, hurricanes, floods, and all the things we call natural disasters or acts of God.

Legally, while the lease is in effect, God cannot interfere with what Satan is doing. That is unless man gives him legal authority to do so! To Satan's horror, he discovered that God had written a covenant clause into the lease. It gave God authority to make covenants with man and to interfere with Satan's plans. The power of the covenant and its disastrous meaning for Satan is seen in the authority over Satan Jesus gave to his disciples.

> Behold! I have given you authority and power to trample upon serpents and scorpions, and physical and mental strength and ability over all the power that the enemy [Satan] possesses; and nothing shall in any way harm you. (Luke 10:19 AMP)

That authority has been passed on to believers. Satan brings and causes disasters. He is our enemy. He is determined to destroy us because believers are very dangerous to him. Jesus implied that if our faith was as big as a mustard seed (Mathew 17:20), we could quiet the storms and defuse the tornadoes.[8] That's why Satan wants to keep us scared, ignorant, and discouraged. His interference in our lives is often experienced as disasters. Satan thinks if he can keep us afraid, he will keep us powerless because fear blocks faith. That's the reason he keeps confronting us with this roll call of the forces arrayed against us. He wants us to think that with all these enemies lined up against us, we don't have a chance.

But God had bigger plans than Satan could dream of. Earth has been invaded, but God uses what Satan intends for evil to serve his ultimate will and purpose. To better understand what God is doing, we revisit the subject of law and order. It keeps everything together and working as it should. Even when it comes to such theoretical areas as antimatter, it is obvious that law and order hold it all together.

We easily understand that in a universe built on law and order, breaking one physical law if that could be done would lead to the immediate annihilation of the universe. Law and order causes everything to cohere. Consider the law of gravity, an immutable law. We can find ways to use it to our advantage, but we can't bend it or break it; it will break us instead. We cannot pretend we are like Superman, immune to the law of gravity, as so many of us did as children, and expect to fly when we jump off a roof.

We expect law and order to also apply to all living things. It's written in the Bible, "The soul that sinneth, it shall die" (Ezekiel 18:4). Satan sinned but didn't die. Adam and Eve sinned but didn't die. So how can rebellious Satan and his hordes of evil be apparently exempt from law and order? Adam and Eve should have experienced God's wrath and been annihilated but weren't. What's going on? Why weren't the malefactors destroyed when they sinned? Logic says that the only way annihilation can be prevented is if a protective shield comes between God's holiness experienced as wrath and anger and the sinner who will be annihilated by it.

This brings us to something that is far more amazing than any saga such as *Star Wars* or *Dune* could imagine. The answer to our questions is simple. In Romans 8:29, we read, "For whom he did foreknow, he also did predestinate to be conformed to the image of his Son, that he might be the firstborn among many brethren." If I understand these words correctly, they tell me God is using Satan and his demons to accomplish a plan he had put into effect before the beginning of time, before Satan was created. God is raising up a family of sons and daughters, and saying yes to Jesus puts our names are on that list!

For God to achieve his purpose, he is protecting us from his wrath while he is conforming us to the image of his Son. There is another statement in the Bible that adds to this picture of God's plan: "For God hath not appointed us to wrath, but to obtain salvation by our Lord Jesus Christ" (1 Thessalonians 5:9). Logic tells us that if we're dealing with a plan laid down prior to creation, there should be a continuous thread relating to it woven throughout the Bible. Does that thread exist? Yes.

The Bible tells us God and man talked together in the garden before the Fall.[9] The reason man was able to have this fellowship and not be destroyed by God's holiness was that he had been made in the image and likeness of God. Whatever the emanation was that was coming from God it was also coming from man. This was lost in the Fall. You could say that in the beginning, Adam and Eve were the most powerful sorcerers ever to live being semi-creators or cocreators with God. Naming the animals was actually defining their characters. In Hebrew, names define the character. Until Adam gave it its character, the dog was only an animated lump of clay.

In the garden following the Fall, Satan was jumping around celebrating his victory. His joy was short-lived. He learned he didn't get a title deed but only a lease. Worse than that, it was a lease with a lot of fine print. God's hidden plan that sent cold shivers down Satan's spine. Before the dust had settled, God began to speak his plan into being.[10] Satan was furious. It wasn't fair! God had changed the battle plan. The next battle would take place on earth, not on God's throne. Instead of helping him defeat God, Satan's slaves would be his worst enemies with power to interfere with him every which way.

No matter what evil plan of deception Satan tries, he finds God is there first. Whatever Satan means for evil, God uses for good. Over and over, God declares that all things were subject to his divine will.

> For I am God, and there is no other; I am God, and there
> is no one like Me, Declaring the end from the beginning
> And from ancient times things which have not been
> done, Saying, "My purpose will be established, And I will
> accomplish all My good pleasure." (Isaiah 46:9–10 AMP)

To his horror, Satan discovered he hadn't been able to shut God out of the earth. God had reserved for himself a door to the world, a direct line of communication and power. That was why God could speak with the man and woman, clothe them, and bless them. That was why God was in control of history. Satan held the lease but had no legal authority to keep God out. Man was subject to the will of the sin master, Satan. But the moment any man turned to God, Satan's power over that man was broken.

It was God who first clothed the man and woman in animal skins; such was his care. In spite of our sinfulness, God loves us just as much as he loves Jesus.[11] His love is so great that he is willing to endure the grief of the despising of his love and the turning away from him of all the angels and men who choose to follow Satan into his kingdom of darkness to have a family that loves him and on whom he can lavish his love. "But as it is written, Eye hath not seen, nor ear heard, neither have entered into the heart of man, the things which God hath prepared for them that love him" (1 Corinthians 2:9).

Paul used two words in Romans 8:29 that help us understand the depth of God's love for us. The first is *foreknow*. One of the best definitions of foreknow is given in Psalm 139:1–3: "O LORD, thou hast searched me, and known me. Thou knowest my downsitting and mine uprising, thou understandest my thought afar off." And again in Jeremiah 1:5, "Before I formed thee in the belly I knew thee; and before thou camest forth out of the womb I sanctified thee."

This is an amazing statement! It means God knows us all. He knows who we are. He knows us all personally; he knows our names and we are not strangers to him. He knows our deepest thoughts, hopes, desires, weaknesses, and strengths. We aren't robots to him but individual persons. We don't have to explain ourselves to him because he already understands us. In a very profound sense, we're his kids, and he's our dad.

He adopted us. "For ye have not received the spirit of bondage again to fear; but ye have received the Spirit of adoption, whereby we cry, Abba [father], Father [dad or daddy]" (Romans 8:15).

God doesn't coerce me into accepting what he offers, but he has predestined me to receive his offer if I'll accept it. That is what the second word, *predestined*, means. He doesn't keep it a secret that he has great things planned for us. His desire to give us his best is what is behind Peter writing in 2 Peter 3:9, "The Lord is not slack concerning his promise, as some men count slackness; but is longsuffering to us–ward, not willing that any should perish, but that all should come to repentance."

Not all will choose to come to repentance, but to those who receive him "gave he power to become the sons of God, even to them that believe on his name" (John 1:12). What happens to those who choose not to love or obey God? Their choice takes them out from under the protection of God's force field. They will experience God's holiness as wrath. It will be by their own choice.

There is no neutral place to hide. We are either in God's kingdom or sin's kingdom. The "wrath of God" is not an emotion. It describes the consequence we experience when we disobey God just as a burned finger is the consequence we feel if we touch a red-hot stove. God, by nature, being the source of law and order, has no choice but to let the consequences of sin (sometimes called his wrath) fall on the sinner if the sinner rejects his gift of grace. By refusing God's gift the sinner commits himself to eternal punishment. God doesn't do the committing. The sinner commits himself. The unholy cannot exist in the presence of the holy. Remember the scene from *Raiders of the Lost Ark* in which the soldiers melted when the ark was opened?

God doesn't force us to choose his family against our will. To give us every opportunity to choose him, he has temporarily suspended the punishment for sin. But the laws are still there; the damage caused by man's disobedience is still there. All creation was thrown into confusion.

> We know that the whole creation has been groaning as
> in the pains of childbirth right up to the present time
> (Romans 8:22 NIV).

Animals, birds, and fish once played and lived together, but they became mortal enemies that ate each other instead of eating the abundant plant life provided for them.

Is it possible to return creation to its pre-sin state and start over without first destroying all who have sinned? God chooses to redeem, not destroy. God's purpose is to restore us to that pre-sin state. God himself pays the ultimate cost of redeeming us by himself bearing "our sins in his own body on the tree, that we, being dead to sins, should live unto righteousness: by whose stripes ye were healed" (1 Peter 2:24). Because God has done this, a day is to come when things will be put back in order.

> The wolf will live with the lamb, the leopard will lie down with the goat, the calf and the lion and the yearling together; and a little child will lead them. The cow will feed with the bear, their young will lie down together, and the lion will eat straw like the ox. The infant will play near the hole of the cobra, and the young child put his hand into the viper's nest. (Isaiah 11:6–8 NIV)

God is building a family. How do you raise a family of millions of sons and daughters all different, all unique, and all of whom must decide for themselves that they want to be in your family? How do you prove to them that you love them and your will for them is good? How do you show them your desire is to bless them with every physical and spiritual blessing? How do you get them to understand they have been called to be lights to the world showing it how much God loves all people? How do you get past their quirkiness and fickleness so they finally realize you're worthy of their praise and devotion? How do you do this at the same time Satan is pulling out all the stops in his efforts to thwart your will? That's what we'll explore next. In the meantime, we need to bring our time machine back to the present.

NOTES

CHAPTER 7

Quirks and Fickleness

In the 1950s, when state universities were still enforcing strict standards of conduct, each dormitory (there were no coed dorms at that time) was overseen by a live-in supervisor, the house mother, assisted by grad students who earned their room and board as section advisors. I was one. My job was to help enforce the rules and to be available if any student needed help. We soon learned our house mother had two quirks we could use to our advantage for the benefit of the students we supervised.

The first was that she loved flattery. We got on her good side by giving her compliments. The second was that you always checked with her secretary before asking her permission for anything. If the house mother was in a good mood, the chances were you would get whatever you wanted. But if she was in a bad mood, she would dig in her heels and you'd never get what you wanted. Her quirks enabled us to manipulate her.

A quirk is a peculiarity of behavior. Children learn how to manipulate their parents' quirks to get what they want. That can be fun and useful. Dad enjoys it when his little girl crawls up on his lap and starts telling him how wonderful he is and how much she loves him because there's something she wants. Mom loves it when children list all the things they will do to get her to say yes to something.

A quirk is like a switch we turn on to get a desired result. Most of the time, we all like having our switches turned on and like turning on other people's switches to get something we desire. Unfortunately, there's a downside. Quirks can be harmful in the sense that some minor action or word can trigger an undesirable response. Sometimes, these bad quirks can lead to very difficult situations.

Fickleness is another matter entirely. It has no good side. A fickle person is unstable in all ways, quick to change opinions, affections, or allegiance, and worst of all, is unreliable. It is very disturbing when the people with whom we live and work turn out to be fickle. It is annoying to have someone say enthusiastically that he or she will do something but never do it. Worse still are politicians who make all kinds of promises to get elected and never keep a single promise. They leave you feeling you have been betrayed.

There is a saying that became popular some years ago: "What's a mother to do?" When we look at the Hebrews and how they acted, we can almost hear God asking, "What's a God to do?" The Hebrews possessed bad quirks and fickleness in abundance. God was constantly battling these two characteristics in them. When we examine a few of the Israelites' quirks and fickleness, we will begin to understand why Jehovah God did some of the things he did. He had to mold and unite the people into a holy nation, a kingdom of priests, but that wasn't easy. "And ye shall be unto me a kingdom of priests, and an holy nation. These are the words which thou shalt speak unto the children of Israel" (Exodus 19:6).

God Uses Quirks and Fickleness

After clothing Adam and Eve and telling them he had a plan to undo the evil they had done, God said, "You must leave my garden." The gates of the garden closed, and a guard was set. From that time on, Adam and Eve lived with the memory of how it had once been. The animals with which they had once talked became wild, without speech, and turning on each other to kill and eat. The ground that had joyously provided food for them and the animals only grudgingly yielded its grain and fruit.

Meanwhile, the promise God had made rang in their ears, and they talked longingly of the day God would redeem them. They told the story of their shame and of God's promise to their children and their children's children. They taught their children how to talk with God. For a thousand years, Adam and Eve repeated the story. Though they talked with God often, he did not reveal any more of his plan.

These conversations between God and Adam and Adam's descendants tell us that they were accustomed to God's voice and knew he loved them and was caring for them. That's why it was some 2,000 years after the Fall that Abram, who lived in Ur of the Chaldeans, knew God's voice. The message Jehovah God spoke to him was exciting. He knew that at long last, God was beginning to put his plan into action. It was the first step toward the redemption God had promised Adam and Eve.

Abram developed into a great a man of faith, but on the way, he was subject to quirks and fickleness. We seem to have a difficult time keeping our hands off what God is doing; we become impatient for him to act especially when we start thinking something's got to be done right now. We end up doing what we think is wise only to discover we've made a mess of things. This was especially true of Abram. Jehovah God had said to Abram, "I will make of you a great nation, and I will bless you with abundant increase of favors and make your name famous and distinguished, and you will be a blessing dispensing good to others" (Genesis 12:2 AMP).

Abram believed God and did as God instructed—most of the time. In the years that followed, however, Abram's fickleness showed up a few times and he got ahead of God. He acted in his own wisdom. Two occasions concerned lying about his wife, Sari, and introducing her as his sister, which in one sense was true.[1] God had to save Sari, who must have been very beautiful, first from Pharaoh and then from King Abimelech. Both men had wanted to wed her. Each time, God intervened and used Abram's fickleness to make Abram richer.

When Abram and Sarah were too old to conceive and bear children, God gave Abraham a son, Isaac. Isaac's birth was a God thing; it was impossible for Abraham or Sarah to take any credit for it. No room for fickleness. It was Isaac's son Jacob who took his family to the land of Goshen in Egypt. Only God could have arranged it. There they lived 400 years and grew in numbers to about two million. Things were pretty quiet during those 400 years. It was when things got tough and they began to cry out to Jehovah God that their quirkiness and fickleness began to show up in full force.

Each of us has quirks. It might be a simple thing as expressed in this silly poem.

I eat my peas with honey,
I've done it all my life.
It makes the peas taste funny,
But it keeps them on the knife!

As that little poem illustrates, quirks are irrational. Though she was intelligent and educated, my aunt had this thing about the brakes on her car. She would stop her car by slowly bumping into a tree. She said she was saving the brakes in case of an emergency.

Many quirks, like my aunt's, are senseless but harmless (unless you're a tree), but others reveal deep flaws of character. Since man was made in the image and likeness of God and as quirkiness in God's nature is a logical impossibility, we are forced to conclude that the quirkiness of our human nature is a result of sin, of our fallen human nature.

God Deals with Fickleness

That we are quirky cannot be denied. That the Hebrews were quirky cannot be denied. But worse than that, they were fickle. That fact helps us understand why God did what he did to them. As God said, they were a "stiff-necked people."[2] Satan used every opportunity to exploit this fault. Fickleness is a good description of the Hebrews as we pick up their story in Goshen after 400 years. They had kept their ethnic purity as well as the belief they were a chosen people according to the promise Jehovah God had given Abraham.

Unfortunately, a pharaoh who did not remember Joseph had come into power. Egged on by Satan's suggestions (implied), the Egyptians looked upon these foreigners, now numbering at least two million and living free in Goshen, as a cheap source of slave labor for the pharaoh's projects. Being reduced from rich visitors to poor and abused slaves, the Hebrews finally remembered they had a God who had chosen them and had looked after them. They cried out to Jehovah, God of Israel.

The trouble was that when each crisis was over, their fickleness kicked in and they forgot God. The story's told about a man who was sliding off a roof and couldn't stop. In desperation, he cried out, "God, if you'll save me I'll do anything you want me to! I'll go to church! I'll tithe!" Just then, his clothes caught on a nail and he was saved. He cried out, "Never mind, God!"

That illustrates the fickle attitude of the Hebrews. When they needed God's help, they were all for worshiping Him and doing whatever He required. Once the crisis passed, however, they forgot Him—until the next crisis. But God was not about to be forgotten. He had a plan to fulfill, a promise to keep. To do it, God used astounding miracles that no man could duplicate.

First, he called Moses and Aaron to deliver his message to the Hebrews in Goshen and to Pharaoh. As Pharaoh dug in his heels and wouldn't let the Hebrews go, God instructed Moses to set loose plague after devastating plague. In the end, the Egyptian people were so desperate to get rid of the Hebrews that they dumped all their wealth on them. The Hebrews arrived at the bank of the Red Sea loaded down with the wealth of Egypt.

We told the story of their escape and crossing the Red Sea in chapter 3. Once they were safely across, they gathered on the bank. They stood and looked out over the sea that drowned the Egyptian army. Moses and the people sang a song of victory.

> I will sing unto the LORD, for he hath triumphed gloriously;
>> the horse and his rider hath he thrown into the sea.
> The LORD is my strength and my song,
>> and he is become my salvation;
> this is my God, and I will praise him,
>> my father's God, and I will exalt him. (Exodus 15:1–2 ESV)

To fully appreciate the magnitude of the miracles that were needed to bring the Hebrews out of Egypt, to cross the sea, and to feed and water them and their cattle as they wandered in the desert, we need to consider the logistics. According to the account in Exodus 14, while the Egyptian army was shrouded in darkness, the Hebrews had light and could cross the sea at night. One estimate is that to do so would require a three-mile-wide gap in the sea. The people would have to walk 5,000 abreast and 400 people deep plus their belongings and cattle. The average walking speed for humans is about three miles per hour. The wall of water on each side would have been twenty or thirty feet high. Can you imagine walking for two hours across the bed of the sea with walls of water looming ominously on each side?

Crossing the sea was not the only logistical problem. Each time they camped at the end of the day, they needed a campground. Some estimate it would have been two-thirds the size of Rhode Island if you allowed ample room for tents and cattle. I believe that's exaggerated, but it does make you think. According to the army's quartermaster general, it would take 1,500 tons of food and 11,000,000 gallons of water each day to take care of that many. Their trek through the desert was a mammoth miracle!

Though the Hebrews had experienced a miraculous escape from Pharaoh, when their stomachs started to growl and they were parched, they realized they couldn't survive on yesterday's miracles. It didn't take long for their fickleness to rise to the surface. Satan was enjoying this discontent and unleashed his demons of complaining, arguing, and whining. Within two days, the Israelites were complaining about their lack of food and water.

That doesn't seem like a logical thing to do. Wouldn't the logical thing in light of their amazing and miraculous deliverance be to excitedly anticipate how God would provide for them? They had witnessed an amazing miracle at the sea, and they had witnessed how they had been spared from all the plagues that had devastated Egypt. In view of all that, their response should have been to thank him in advance for his provision.

But that wasn't their response. They didn't have the patience to trust God to do what he had promised. They thought that they had it coming to them by rights and that God was dragging his feet. I'm sure Satan's seductive forces were hard at work planting discontent in the Hebrews' minds and egging them on. Trust was not in their vocabulary; complaining was.

Something happened when they arrived at Mount Sinai that was very important; it changed everything and explains many things. Remember, these people weren't hearing from God for the first time; they had their family history that started with Abraham and the promises of blessing

God had given him. They knew how God had made Abraham rich and promised that his descendants would be blessed as well.

They knew how God had sent Joseph ahead to secure Goshen where they would live in peace while they grew in numbers. They probably never would have ventured to the Promised Land if Pharaoh hadn't taken away their riches and enslaved them. When they got to Mount Sinai, Moses went up to talk to God. He received a message for the house of Jacob. More of God's master plan was unfolded. He had set these people aside for a special mission. He told them why they had been set apart. Jehovah instructed Moses,

> Tell the children of Israel; Ye have seen what I did unto the Egyptians, and how I bare you on eagles' wings, and brought you unto myself. Now therefore, if ye will obey my voice indeed, and keep my covenant, then ye shall be a peculiar treasure unto me above all people: for all the earth is mine: And ye shall be unto me a kingdom of priests, and an holy nation. (Exodus 19:3–6)

Can't you hear the people saying, "Boy! I knew we were special, but I had no idea we were that special! Jehovah just said he wants us to rule the whole world for him. Man, what a deal! Of course we accept. We're going to rule the world!"

There was a catch to this they managed to overlook, which we will see in a moment. You may wonder how they got the idea they would rule the world. History offers many examples, but think about the Roman Empire. Caesar dwelt in Rome and ruled his empire through governors in all the provinces. In Egypt, the situation was similar except that it was the priests who exerted a lot of control even over the pharaoh.

Is it any wonder that "all the people answered together, and said, 'All that the LORD hath spoken we will do'"[3] When you were a kid, did your dad ever hold out a crisp, ten-dollar bill to you and ask, "How would you like to have this?" As you started to reach for it, he pulled it back and said, "Wait. There's something you'll have to do first." Suddenly, that ten-dollar bill doesn't look so attractive. You think twice about how badly you want it.

This is what the Israelites had overlooked. They really didn't hear when God said, "Obey my voice and keep my covenant." But God meant what He said, and from that point on, Jehovah God's goal was to develop this nation into a kingdom of priests, a holy nation to be a light to the Gentiles.[4] As descendants of Abraham, they had the correct lineage to be a kingdom of priests, but they lacked the experience, the schooling that develops character and would have qualified them to rule.

J.R.R. Tolkien's trilogy *The Lord of the Rings*[5] gives us an excellent example of what it means to go to school to become qualified to assume the role of a kingdom of priests, a holy nation. In Tolkien's story, a young man, Aragorn, born of the lineage of kings, was forced to be an unknown wanderer. He longed for the day when the dark enemy would be defeated and the crown of his ancestors would rightfully be placed on his head.

The road to that day was long and hard. He had to fight many battles and win the love and loyalty of those over whom he would be king for he couldn't be their king without their consent. He had to fight great battles against great powers of evil. When the war was won and the last battle fought, he had defeated the enemy and had won the hearts of the people just as he had won the hearts of those who had fought beside him. He had earned the right to be their king.

The problem with the Israelites was that even though the people agreed with being a kingdom of priests and said that was what they wanted to do, they kept rebelling at every step. They did not want to go to school; they wanted all the benefits and privileges without earning them.

As we pick up the story again, we learn how much of a pain to God man's quirks and fickleness could be. God promised Abraham that his descendants would be greatly blessed and prospered. That did not include going back to what the Hebrews referred to as the fleshpots of Egypt or returning to slavery and oppression; it meant moving forward, acting on the Word of God, and obeying him. Obey and possess. Disobey and be dispossessed.

Logic tells us that these people should have been whooping it up. They had the deal of deals going for them, and all they had to do was trust, obey, and move forward. That's where the deal started to break down. It was going to take effort, training, and maturing on their part, and they didn't like that at all. The stubborn Hebrews refused to do their part. In spite of all the miracles, they refused to trust. They kept demanding that God prove himself. In their minds, it wasn't their trust that needed to be proven. It wasn't they who needed to act; it was God who needed to prove himself. Such was their fickleness. They were all for being a kingdom of priests one day and then wanting to return to slavery the next.

> And the whole congregation of the children of Israel murmured against Moses and Aaron in the wilderness: And the children of Israel said unto them, Would to God we had died by the hand of the LORD in the land of Egypt, when we sat by the flesh pots, and when we did eat bread to the full; for ye have brought us forth into this wilderness, to kill this whole assembly with hunger. (Exodus 16:2–4)

These Hebrews were so stubborn that they had a hard time obeying the simplest command such as, "Gather twice as much manna on the sixth day so that you will have manna to eat on the seventh day." First, they tried hoarding it during the week, but it spoiled. Then they were too lazy to gather enough on the sixth day and so had none stored up for the Sabbath. It caused God to ask, "How long refuse ye to keep my commandments and my laws?"[6] We see this same quirkiness at Mount Sinai. God descended to the top of Mount Sinai. There was no question but what this was Jehovah, the I AM THAT I AM of Exodus 3:14.

> Then Moses brought the people out of the camp to meet God, and they took their stand at the foot of the mountain. Now Mount Sinai was wrapped in smoke because the LORD had descended on it in fire. The smoke of it went up like the smoke of a kiln, and the whole mountain trembled greatly. And as the sound of the trumpet grew louder and louder, Moses spoke, and God answered him in thunder. The LORD came down on Mount Sinai, to the top of the mountain. And the LORD called Moses to

the top of the mountain, and Moses went up. (Exodus 19:17–20 ESV)

The dramatic displays of Jehovah God's presence, his acts and miracles, had always come about with Moses acting as God's spokesman. The people were becoming very concerned. Moses had been gone over a month. Impatience and uncertainty began to take over their minds. Since God had called them to be a kingdom of priests, they assumed that meant they were already a wise people, so they applied their wisdom to the situation. It seemed certain Moses wasn't coming back. They reasoned they needed some other way of ensuring God would be in their midst.

Jehovah God had called them, led them out of Egypt, and said they were to possess the Promised Land. How could that happen without his presence to lead them? How could Jehovah God be present to lead them without Moses? Moses was their connection with Jehovah God, but Moses was gone. What could they do? In as much as the cloud of smoke was still on the top of Mount Sinai, it was obvious God was still there. They needed to act before the cloud left. They reasoned, "What if we make Jehovah a place to sit in our midst? Perhaps then he will consent to go with us."[7]

They decided to make a golden calf on which Jehovah could sit. That idea isn't as far-fetched as it may sound. When Jehovah gave Moses fabrication instructions for the tabernacle, in those instructions were the plans for a seat for Jehovah: "You shall make a mercy seat of pure gold … There I will meet with you" (Exodus 25:17, 22 ESV).

Having made up their minds that they wanted a golden calf to replace Moses, a small group of the "enlightened" people begged Aaron to make them a golden calf on which God could ride. Aaron did not intend the calf to be a worshiped idol but Jehovah's seat. This is borne out by the words Aaron spoke after sculpting the golden calf: "And when Aaron saw it, he built an altar before it; and Aaron made proclamation, and said, 'Tomorrow is a feast to the LORD [Jehovah]'" (Exodus 32:5).

The feast Aaron was proclaiming was to Jehovah, not to worship the golden calf. Again, Satan was working to destroy God's plan. I do not mean he was visibly there. His deeds of evil are done in secret by planting ideas in people's minds.

Some in the encampment were ready to embrace Satan's temptations to worship false gods and engage in all manner of drunkenness and sexual sin. The phrase "rise up to play" suggests sex-play in Hebrew.[8] They chose to worship false gods and put them before Jehovah. The question was, how will God deal with this satanic invasion? Were these sinners real Jews or people just along for the ride? Regardless of who they were, their presence was a small amount of leaven that leavened the whole loaf. They were the bad apple that spoils the bunch. Their teachings and beliefs could end up corrupting all the Hebrews. Jesus warned his disciples about false leaven: "He bade them not beware of the leaven of bread, but of the doctrine of the Pharisees and of the Sadducees" (Matthew 16:12).

How does God deal with this? He takes very logical steps. First, he has to get rid of the bad apples as he cannot allow the worship of false gods or allow those who practice such worship to have any influence over the rest. Second, he has to teach the people that though they could not see him, he knew what they were doing. Third, it was another opportunity to demonstrate not just his sovereignty but also his wrath and anger at disobedience and whoring after other gods. Logic says that to get this point across, the penalty for disobedience would need to be as clear cut and unalterable as "If you touch a hot stove, you'll be burned."

The steps taken were very drastic indeed. First, Moses turned the golden calf into fine powder, spread it on the water, and made the people drink it. Powdered gold makes a strong laxative! Those who had never embraced Jehovah as their God and had always been devoted to Satan's false gods had to be destroyed to prevent contamination. Moses sent the Levites throughout the camp to slay all those who were guilty, about 3,000. God blotted these demon worshipers out of his book.[9] Though the people witnessed this, though they knew God was watching them, they continued to be stiff-necked.[10]

After Moses had given them the Law and they had constructed the tabernacle where Jehovah would dwell in their midst, three men, Korah, Dathan, and Abiram, along with 250 princes and leaders of the congregation came to Moses and Aaron and announced,

> Enough of you! This whole congregation is holy. You're
> no better than any of us. Where do you come off setting

yourselves up above us, making yourself our prince? You
haven't brought us to a land of milk and honey, or fields
rich in crops and vineyards full of grapes. All you've
brought us to is more sand.[11]

Complaining like that was not smart. First, Jehovah made the ground
open and swallow the three ringleaders with all their families and
possessions. Then he sent out a fire and killed all 250 leaders as they stood
there. The point is simple. They knew from the beginning that Jehovah
was using Moses, with whom he talked directly. They knew they had
begged Jehovah not to talk to them directly as they were scared of him.[12]

They suddenly thought they were so smart that they could tell
Jehovah what to do and take over Moses's leadership! Trust did not come
easy for these people; complaining did. When you have an enemy like
Satan filling your head with doubts about how God is running things
combined with pride in your wisdom, you're headed for trouble. At times,
it can seem far easier to go back to the fleshpots of Egypt than to step
out in trust.

God's solution to forming these bedraggled people into a united
and holy nation may not be to our taste. But could he have logically and
realistically done anything different given what he had to work with?
That's the tough question. How do you deal with quirks and fickleness?
Consider this example. When it came time to enter and possess the
Promised Land, they sent twelve spies who came back with a good report
as to what the land was like. But ten of them reported that they could
never win a battle with the inhabitants even though Jehovah had said he
would deliver the inhabitants into their hands.

Jehovah's response was to tell them they would all die in the desert.
Only their children would be the ones to go in and possess the land. Their
response to Jehovah's sentence was to say, "Okay, we get the point. We're
ready to go right now. Lead the way, Moses." To which Jehovah said, "No!
You've had your chance. You've been nothing but trouble since I brought
you out of Egypt. Your punishment is that you will die in the desert and
never see the Promised Land."[13]

NOTES

CHAPTER 8

Birth Paroxysms

Imagine you're one of a select group of a dozen world leaders each with different histories, backgrounds, and beliefs. In deference to the fact that each of you is equally important and qualified, you're at a round table; no one seat is more important than the others. Your task is to come up with a plan that will prove to the world that there is only one God who is over all and in all and through all. This is not a God to be trifled with or ignored. He demands holiness and rewards it with blessings. He punishes sin.

Can you and your fellow experts devise a plan to accomplish this task? It will not take you long to realize there is little possibility of twelve people coming to consensus. It's as if everyone in an orchestra fancies himself the conductor with his individual style that is in contrast to and conflicts with the others. The resultant music played simultaneously by all as each one thinks it should be played will be nothing more than nerve-racking discord.

We are forced by this dilemma to seek for one who is eminently more qualified than all twelve world leaders put together. If twelve cannot agree, how do we get two million people to agree? That is the situation facing Jehovah God. What will God do? What is his solution to this problem?

We have already seen that to show how serious his relationship is with Israel, it cannot be treated in a haphazard or halfhearted way. Drastic measures are called for. God will need to take extreme measures to embed the knowledge of who he is indelibly in their minds and hearts. This is what you would logically expect from a God who is holy.

Up to this point, logic has led us to draw two conclusions. First, God is a God of law and order. For that reason, the fact that the wages of sin (rebellion) is death is something God can't arbitrarily change. To break his laws would result in annihilation of himself because evil and holiness cannot coexist.

Second, no matter how strong God's love is, it doesn't allow him to make exceptions to his laws or break them. Though God isn't willing for any man to perish, the law is the law and cannot be broken. To all appearances, that's bad news for us all. We can't work our way out of this one. The law is the law. Our only response must be "Good-bye! We're going down!" But wait. Nobody went down.

The Secret Plan

When Adam and Eve should have been disintegrating into nothing as did the enemy in *Raiders of the Lost Ark* when the ark's lid was opened, they didn't! Instead, God revealed he had a plan written into creation before creation had begun.[1] That plan, we are told, was good news for us! Man, who lost his clothing of glory, stood naked, exposed. But instead of wrath coming from God, man experienced a great love. God made clothes to cover their nakedness by sacrificing animals they once loved and perhaps talked with. While he did so, God gave them a word of encouragement, just a hint about his secret plan he was not setting motion. It is important to remember that prior to this, Satan had no clue that God had a secret plan. This news disturbed him greatly.

Satan didn't expect to hear that men, his legal slaves, would become his worst enemies.[2] That infuriated him. It wasn't supposed to happen! Just from what we've learned about him so far, we know that Satan, in response to this news, wouldn't sit around pouting and doing nothing. Believing himself so much smarter than God, the instant he learned God had a secret plan, he began making new plans of his own. He was not going to let God get away with this. He would exert all his powers to thwart God at every turn, wrench the ownership of this earth out of

God's hands, and rebuild his army for the battle that would take place on earth.

God, of course, knew what Lucifer would be like and would try if he rebelled and turned into Satan. That is why God was able to take what Satan meant for evil and use it for good. Likewise, God knew man, his creation. Just as nothing Satan did caught God by surprise, nothing man did caught God by surprise. That was why God was very deliberate in what he did. God acted in such a way that there would be no question that he was in control. All Satan's attempts at opposition and disruption became opportunities for God to demonstrate his superior power.

The new sinful nature that man had acquired included a natural inclination to be stubborn, intractable, and nonresponsive to the guiding of God and the Holy Spirit. This was compounded by Satan's constant interference. We have already seen an example of that in the rebellion of the Hebrews after their liberation from slavery. For these reasons, each step of the nation-building process required God to intervene supernaturally. The behavior of the Hebrews was not the kind of stuff out of which you can mold a holy nation, but that was what God was doing.

His intervention is always in the form of miracles beyond the ability of any man to duplicate. Abraham and Sarah have no children until Isaac is born. Isaac's birth was a miracle because Abraham was 100 and Sarah's womb had dried up. Abraham's faith is further tested when God tells him to offer Isaac as a sacrifice. By this time, Abraham's faith in God has matured so that

> By faith Abraham ... while the testing of his faith was still in progress, had already brought Isaac for an offering; he who had gladly received and welcomed God's promises was ready to sacrifice his only son, Of whom it was said, Through Isaac shall your descendants be reckoned. For he reasoned that God was able to raise him up even from among the dead. (Hebrews 11:17–19 AMP)

From this starting point of Abraham's great faith, look at the logical sequence of what God is doing. God unfolded each step of his plan with a supernatural miracle. This eliminated any possibility that man could claim the Hebrew faith was man-made. This is a distinguishing mark of the Bible and its claim to be God's revelation of himself. When it was time for God to raise up a leader to lead his people out of Egypt, Satan stepped in and had all the male babies of all the Hebrews slain at birth. God arranged for Moses to escape and even be raised under Satan's nose by Pharaoh's daughter.

In Goshen, the Hebrews multiplied greatly. God's task of molding them into a holy nation had grown enormously. We couldn't get twelve people to come to consensus. God was faced with the task of molding two million intractable people into a holy nation. God's first step in the molding process was to deliver them from Egypt with such a show of supernatural power and blessing that all the nations around as well as the Hebrews would have to admit that only Jehovah God could have done it.

The first show of power was the plagues that fell on Egypt and not on the Hebrews in Goshen. God told Moses that was to prove to Pharaoh that the God of the Hebrews was the one true God. This was followed by the miraculous parting of the water to let the Hebrews cross the Red Sea and the drowning of Pharaoh's army when the waters flowed back.

Unfortunately, the magnitude of that deliverance lost its impact in the minds of the Hebrews in only a few days because Satan was at work. The people were willing to complain, and Satan was willing to help them. Satan suggested that delivering them from Egypt was God's idea, not an answer to their pleas. That meant that it was God's responsibility to clothe and feed them. They complained because in their minds, God wasn't doing it fast enough. Then they complained because they didn't like the menu![3]

The people did rejoice when they learned that God had called them to be a holy nation of priests. They thought that meant they would rule the world. They rejoiced until they discovered there was a man side as well as a God side to being a chosen people. Nevertheless, God continued to instruct and mold them. We've already seen what happened to the tribal units that had chosen idolatry. Idolaters and their blasphemous teachings had to be obliterated. God removed his protective covering from them, and they were destroyed by his wrath. God was jealously guarding the Hebrew faith he was establishing. He set before the people rituals, feasts, and sacrifices designed as teaching tools that had to be observed and kept pure. These are not for appeasing him but to aid the Hebrews in keeping fresh their memories of his great acts and to prepare them for his greatest gift of love, Jesus.

The School of Obedience

Do not think life under God's covenant is a wearisome burden; that would be illogical because it would be contrary to God's nature as revealed by his created universe. There are tremendous benefits that come from observing God's rituals, feasts and sacrifices. Those benefits were first spelled out by God in Leviticus 26:3–13. Micah described the benefits as an idyllic life of prosperity free from fear (Micah 4:4). To put it in today's vernacular, stay true to God and you will be blessed out of your socks!

As discussed in chapter 4, God put a force field around the Israelites inside which they were safe and blessed. My parents looked after me and kept me secure and blessed. They took me fun places and did fun things with me. But boy, if I talked back to them and told them what I would and wouldn't do, I unleashed their wrath!

It was something like that with the Hebrews. The force field could be weakened by disobedience. It could get holes in it that let God's wrath and anger through. God goes to great pains to explain the curses that get through when the force field is weakened and gets holes in it. It was like that with my parents. They used to tell me what I could do to "earn" a spanking. Failure to obey them was one guaranteed way!

The Hebrews had to keep their faith pure or there would be no force field of protection and blessing. Without the force field, Israel could never enter the Promised Land or fulfill its mission of being a light to the world.[4] It is logical to conclude that God could not tolerate anything that threatened to weaken or destroy Israel's faith. Objects of idol worship, people who had sold out to Satan, and animals and anything that had been dedicated to Satan (via false gods) had to be destroyed.

There could be no compromise, no toleration of evil or anything unholy or they would pay dearly. They had to understand that only the grace of God kept them from being destroyed. They had to understand that rebellion was as bad as witchcraft.[5] At the same time, they had to learn that obedience brought blessings, prosperity, and favor with their enemies.[6]

The destruction of Jericho is an interesting example of God's supernatural power and the destructiveness of sin. Jericho's walls were supposed to be impenetrable, but all the Hebrew army had to do was march around the walls once each day for six days and seven times on the seventh day. At end of the seventh march on the seventh day, they shouted and the walls were pushed down except for the section of wall where the harlot Rahab lived with her family. She had protected and saved the lives of the two spies Joshua had sent to Jericho.

Archeologists have discovered that the walls were literally pushed to the ground filling the ditches creating a level ramp. The Israelite army was able to walk straight across the ramp and into the city without climbing over a huge mound rubble.[7] They also discovered that the portion of wall where Rahab lived had been left standing. There was no question but that this was a supernatural feat of God. That story in itself would be enough to put the fear of God into the hearts of the surrounding nations.

The Israelites were told that the city was accursed and the people were enemies of God. They were told to destroy the city and all its inhabitants except for Rahab and her family. Only the gold and silver were to be saved and brought into the treasury of the Lord. They were to keep themselves from everything that was accursed (dedicated to the worship of false gods) lest they themselves become accursed.

Joshua's fame spread, as did the fear of his army. From Satan's point of view, this was getting out of hand. He found a rebel in the person of Achan. Achan's mutinous behavior caused the force field to be weakened. The army had become accustomed to God delivering their enemies into its hands. Unaware that Achan had done something to weaken the force field, they asked Joshua if they could take just a token army to capture the nation city of Ai. Joshua agreed.

The battle didn't go well; the small army returned having suffered severe losses. Joshua rent his clothes and sought the Lord, crying that at that rate, the Canaanites and others would annihilate the Hebrews. God told Joshua that his army had been defeated because there was sin in the camp. This event demonstrated the necessity of purity to stay under the force field of God's blessing. Achan, yielding to a spirit of lust, had snitched a few of the things from Jericho that should have been destroyed. That put a big hole in the force field and was why they began to lose their battles.[8]

Achan's evil cost the lives of good soldiers; it cost him his life, the lives of his family, and his livestock. The force field was mended. Achan's treachery had started to cause Israel much damage. He had become the personification of the evil of Jericho. Like a deadly cancer, the evil had to be removed along with every tentacle and root. He was removed. The force field was mended. Ai was destroyed.

How Can a Loving God Command Genocide?

As we think about these stories, our minds try to rationalize God's command to destroy human life with the definition of a loving God. In our minds, it doesn't compute. We have no problem with cutting out a cancer that threatens to destroy us, but we are appalled at the idea of comparing people to cancer. Let's see if we can find a logical answer that satisfies. We begin by piecing together several verses of scripture. The first is from a message the apostle Paul delivered to the Gentiles in Antioch in which he quoted from the prophet Isaiah.

> For so the Lord has charged us, saying, I have set you to be a light for the Gentiles (the heathen), that you may bring eternal salvation to the uttermost parts of the earth. (Acts 13:47 AMP)

> I the Lord have called You (the Messiah) for a righteous purpose and in righteousness; I will take You by the hand and will keep You; I will give You for a covenant to the people (Israel), for a light to the nations (Gentiles). (Isaiah 42:6 AMP)

Paul expressed the same message in his letter to the Christians in Rome when he stated that God had designed Israel to be the tame olive vine onto which the rest of the world, the wild olive shoots, were to be engrafted. He reminded us that it was the root, Israel, that supported us.[9]

These two passages appear to make genocide illogical. The people he has destroyed are the very ones he wanted to save! We can see the logic in selecting a chosen people to be like the root of a tame olive tree, but the people God had chosen were anything but perfect. That makes it difficult to understand how God could achieve his plan, but he did when he sent his Son.

Paul called us wild olives who were grafted onto that root when we become Christians. This arrangement is very good for us; it puts us in the direct line of recipients of all the promises made to Abraham because we are now his heirs.[10] Peter seconded what Paul said.

> The Lord does not delay and is not tardy or slow about what He promises, according to some people's conception of slowness, but He is long-suffering (extraordinarily patient) toward you, not desiring that any should perish, but that all should turn to repentance. (2 Peter 3:9 AMP)

This brings us back to that sticky question, why did God command genocide? It does seem illogical in view of Peter's statement that those were the people Jesus came to save. Logic says there has to be a logical reason. What are we missing? We can make a case that the genocidal cleansing of the Hebrew race was for the purpose of establishing a holy nation and pounding it into their heads that holiness was serious business. We can make a case that supernatural conquest and annihilation of a people would proclaim to the surrounding nations that the Hebrews' God was vastly superior to all their idols and gods.

Neither of these answers is satisfactory. The answer lies elsewhere. The answer lies in the question: Who has your heart? Whom do you worship and serve? To whom have you given your allegiance? God said that certain peoples were his enemies. They would not be enemies unless they had deliberately chosen to be so. You can't become an enemy by accident or ignorance; the only way you can become an enemy of God is by deliberately giving your allegiance to Satan. For many, just like their leader, Satan, there is no turning back; they are incapable of repenting.

Moses made it clear that because of their enmity to God and their wickedness, God delivered his enemies into the hands of the Hebrews to be slain. It had nothing to do with the Hebrews being a wonderful, obedient, God-fearing people because they weren't.

> Do not say in your mind and heart, after the Lord your God has thrust them out from before you, It is because of my righteousness that the Lord has brought me in to possess this land—whereas it is because of the wickedness of these nations that the Lord is dispossessing them before you. Not for your righteousness or for the uprightness of your minds and hearts do you go to possess their land; but because of the wickedness of these nations the Lord your God is driving them out before you, and that He may fulfill the promise which the Lord swore to your fathers, Abraham, Isaac, and Jacob. Know therefore that the Lord your God does not give you this good land to possess because of your righteousness, for you are a hard and stubborn people. (Deuteronomy 9:4–6 AMP)

Word quickly spread about how the Hebrews' God was giving them many mighty victories and no one could stand before them. One would think that the logical thing to do when you learn that your idols are false and that you are no match for the God of Israel would be to make peace with Israel's God. That didn't happen. There was no repentance in Ai, nor was there repentance and turning to Israel's God on the part of the kings beyond Jordan. Instead, they had deliberately chosen to be enemies of Jehovah God. In defiance of Jehovah God, they banded together to oppose Israel and for that paid a heavy price—their destruction and annihilation.[11]

They are, as Paul said, without excuse.[12] In view of this, we see the logic in the annihilation of people who were obviously enemies of God. Otherwise, they would be a constant source of trouble for the Hebrews. Like the rotten apple that spoils the bunch; they would have been a pollutant to Israel's faith.

This answer doesn't quite satisfy because it's still hard for us to believe that every single person was God's enemy. Knowing that God is just and that he is no respecter of persons[13] leads us to conclude that even those who were annihilated in this way would be given one last opportunity to choose for God or against God. Those who choose for God will inherit the kingdom prepared for them.[14] What God has prepared is far superior and greatly to be desired; premature physical death (genocide) just gets us there quicker. We will discover in the end that God's justice is most satisfactory.

Through the above examples, we have seen how God performed miracles to mold the Hebrews into a nation empowered to possess the Promised Land. The miracles could not be explained by natural means, nor could any man take credit for them.

Even when the disobedient Hebrews were taken captive to other countries, Jehovah never let them forget he was God of gods and King of kings. Nor did God let their captors forget that. Even the great king of Babylon, Nebuchadnezzar, had to learn that he was not God and not worthy of worship. He had come to regard himself as the supreme ruler of the whole earth, a god king. Apparently, he had many flaws.

God warned him in a dream to mend his ways. Daniel warned him to repent and begin showing mercy and lovingkindness to the poor and oppressed. The king didn't. As he stood bragging about his power, a voice spoke to him from heaven: Your

> kingdom has departed from you, And you shall be driven from among men and your dwelling will be with the living creatures of the field. You will be made to eat grass like the oxen, and seven times (or years) shall pass over you until you have learned and know that the Most High (God) rules in the kingdom of men and gives it to whomever He will.

At the end of the seven years, Nebuchadnezzar's mind returned to him and he declared,

> Now I, Nebuchadnezzar, praise and extol and honor the King of heaven, Whose works are all faithful and right and Whose ways are just. And those who walk in pride He is able to abase and humble" (Daniel 4:31–32, 34 AMP).

These stories of miracles, deliverance, and victories were all part of going to school! This is what the Israelites had a hard time accepting. They enjoyed the victories and the spoils, but they didn't like having to be obedient to Jehovah and his laws. They had to earn the right to become a kingdom of priests. It didn't come on a silver platter just because they were of the lineage of Abraham; they had to earn it. Before the God part could come, they had to do the man part. Israel couldn't become a kingdom of priests until it had earned the right. The strain, stress, and pain they endured to become a holy nation is like the convulsions a mother experiences when giving birth. When it is done, there is joy.[15]

NOTES

CHAPTER 9

Fasts, Celebrations, and Sacrifices

I look everywhere. I carefully clear everything off my workbench but can't find it. I crawl around with my trouble light looking in every crack and corner. It's only a little spring, probably worth fifteen cents at the most. Isn't it funny how a little spring can make a $1,200 VCR inoperable? Or how an expensive pair of designer glasses can lie in pieces because a little screw is lost?

Many things are like my lost spring. By themselves, they seem insignificant, unimportant. But when you fit them into the places where they belong, their importance becomes clear. That's the case with the three things we'll deal with in this chapter—fasts, celebrations, and sacrifices—activities Jehovah instructed the Israelites to observe.

To understand their importance, let's review some things covered in previous chapters. We learned that prior to the Fall, God had built into creation a secret plan to redeem man. Satan instigated and engineered the Fall and thought he would thereby have all the slave labor he needed for his next attack on Jehovah God's throne.

When Jehovah God revealed he had a plan, Satan realized that if he was to make any headway with his plans, he had to get man to ignore if not forget God and God's plans. That would be difficult. It seems Jehovah God had already done something else. "'For as a belt is bound round a man's waist, so I bound the whole house of Israel and the whole house of

Judah to me,' declares the LORD, 'to be my people for my renown and praise and honour'" (Jeremiah 13:11 NIV).

Everything Satan does is to glorify his name and make it known throughout the earth. It never works. Every attempt Satan made to glorify himself became an opportunity for God to show himself more powerful and more worthy of praise. God's name, his reputation, was on the line. This was not to prove himself to man; it was to win man's allegiance, devotion, and love. He did it because of his great love for us.[1]

In verse after verse, we find God stressing his faithfulness, his fulfilling of his promises, and his mighty acts so his name would be declared throughout the earth. He will not allow his name and what it represents to be profaned. His name will be glorified. This knowledge was the basis for the Israelites' crying to God for help: "Help us, O God of our salvation, for the glory of thy name: and deliver us, and purge away our sins, for thy name's sake" (Psalm 79:9).

Everything God did for the Israelites was done for his name's sake, not theirs.

> Therefore say unto the house of Israel, Thus saith the Lord GOD; I do not this for your sakes, O house of Israel, but for mine holy name's sake, which ye have profaned among the heathen, whither ye went. And I will sanctify my great name, which was profaned among the heathen, which ye have profaned in the midst of them; and the heathen shall know that I am the LORD, saith the Lord GOD, when I shall be sanctified in you before their eyes. (Ezekiel 36:22–23)

Imagine you're the father of an extremely rebellious son. You've done everything you could to bless your son and show him you love him. How would you feel if your son never recognized you as his father and instead ran off after other "fathers," spent all his time with them, and never so much as said hello to you? That is, until he gets himself into piles of trouble and deep in debt and lands in jail. He suddenly remembers you.

He calls and asks you to come and get him out of trouble. He speaks words of repentance but only to get your help. He may think he means them, but you know as soon as everything is going well again, he will once again forsake you for his other "fathers." You have grieved over his conduct, but you'd still do everything you could to help him. That's sort of how it is with Jehovah God.

To help keep these stiff-necked, rebellious people focused on who they were and their destiny, Jehovah God set in place little must-do deeds similar in purpose to the little spring in my VCR. These must-dos are fasts, celebrations, and sacrifices. When they remembered them and remembered their calling, they prospered. When they forgot them, nothing worked for them and trouble came calling.

The first reminder was fasting. Why would anyone want to go without eating or drinking? Maybe once in a while, the food is bad or the coffee tastes like burned rubber, but to deliberately choose not to eat or drink when the food is exquisite and the drink refreshing? There had better be a good reason for that. There is. Fasting is a way of owning up, being honest, and humbling ourselves before God. It's done deliberately to become malleable and allow God to transform us and use us. It releases the power of God into a situation.

An example of its power is seen in Esther, who, with all the Jews, fasted for three days that she might find favor with the king. In finding favor, she prevented the destruction of the Jews.[2] Another example is seen in Moses, who fasted forty days and nights before receiving the covenant between God and Israel.[3]

Next come celebrations. We love celebrations. Give us a reason and we'll party because celebrations are always joyful times. They are about remembering something important that happened to us or about an event that is happening. God had given them a reason to celebrate, and he wanted them to remember that reason and rejoice in it every year. It is the event called the Passover.

The Passover was the pivotal event that caused Pharaoh to give Israel permission to leave Egypt. On that eventful night, the Israelites followed a series of instructions that included killing male lambs and goats. There was nothing unusual in that as that is what they always did in preparing food. But that time, they were to dip hyssop into the blood of the animals and sprinkle the doorposts of their homes with it. It became a line of protection around them. When the angel of death came, it could not cross that line and so passed over their homes on its way to strike dead the firstborn of the Egyptians. This event, including the food they prepared, their dress, and retelling the story was to be observed every year by each family.

> And this day shall be unto you for a memorial; and ye shall keep it a feast to the LORD throughout your generations; ye shall keep it a feast by an ordinance forever ... And ye shall observe the feast of unleavened bread; for in this selfsame day have I brought your armies out of the land of Egypt: therefore shall ye observe this day in your generations by an ordinance forever. (Exodus 12:14, 17)

The giving of the Ten Commandments was the next if not most important event. It was not included in the celebrations. Instead, it was incorporated in the daily life of the people in the form of what is called the *shema*. "Hear, O Israel: the Lord our God is one Lord the only Lord. And you shall love the Lord your God with all your mind and heart and with your entire being and with all your might" (Deuteronomy 6:4–5 AMP). It is the first and greatest commandment. It is fixed to the doorpost of every home and is touched each time a person enters or leaves. Second only to that is the second commandment: "You shall love your neighbor as yourself."[4] These two sum up the whole law.[5] Man has great difficulty in keeping things simple. Soon, a whole body of interpretations and laws grew up around them. God was saying, "Once a year, I want you to go back to the basics."

Next, God listed three annual festivals they were to observe—the Feast of Unleavened Bread, the Feast of Harvest, and the Feast of Ingathering. The Feast of Unleavened Bread celebrates the days of the Exodus. As they were escaping from slavery, they didn't have time to add leaven to their flour and wait for it to rise. It was a time for remembering who they were, where they had come from, and who had delivered them.

The Feast of Harvest was a celebration of the first fruits of their crops. It was a thanksgiving to God for the spring crops. The Feast of Ingathering was a time of giving thanks for the crops that had been harvested. These celebrations centered around the temple and celebrated the promises God had made to them.

> And ye shall serve the LORD your God, and he shall bless thy bread, and thy water; and I will take sickness away from the midst of thee. There shall nothing cast their young, nor be barren, in thy land: the number of thy days I will fulfill. (Exodus 23:25–26)

Last of all come sacrifices. Sacrifices can be a good thing. You can win baseball games with sacrifice flies and bunts. Sacrifice means to purposely give up something or to do something to help achieve a greater good such as winning a game.

Parents make sacrifices for their children. Military people sacrifice their lives for their country. People starting out in a new business make personal sacrifices of time and of doing without to put every penny and resource into their businesses. Sacrifices are good in that they can make many other good things possible.

The sacrifices in the Bible center on a serious, life-threatening problem faced by man. Man was under a death sentence. God wanted to keep foremost in their minds that there was a price to pay for sin. For the price of a bite of fruit, Adam gave up his rulership of the world and delivered the world, himself, and his descendants into the sin master's hands. The soul that sins, it shall die.[6] No apology, no act of repentance can undo it. Death is by the shedding of blood because the life is in the blood.[7]

Among the instructions Moses and some of Israel's elders brought back from the mountain were two instructions concerning a sin offering and a ransom. God was providing a temporary fix to the sin problem in the form of a yearly sin offering. By virtue of this offering, man could choose to be free from sin. This temporary fix was built around animal sacrifices. Why animal sacrifices? The first part of the answer is in Leviticus 17:11: "For the life of the flesh is in the blood." This obvious fact was first made abundantly clear when Cain slew Abel.

> And he [God] said, What hast thou done? the voice of thy brother's blood crieth unto me from the ground. And

now art thou cursed from the earth, which hath opened
her mouth to receive thy brother's blood from thy hand.
(Genesis 4:10–11)

Once Abel's blood had flowed out of him, his life force was gone.
People who are near death from other causes can recover; not so with the
loss of blood. When it goes, there is no coming back.

For the life of the flesh is in the blood: and I have given
it to you upon the altar to make an atonement for your
souls: for it is the blood that maketh an atonement
[ransom, purge away], for the soul (Leviticus 17:10–12).

The sacrifices in Leviticus were to keep the people aware of the
consequences of sin, to ransom them from the consequences of sin, and to
point to a coming Redeemer. It was not a permanent solution; it had to be
repeated each year. The sacrifices looked forward to the day when Jesus
would be the lamb without blemish sacrificed to permanently redeem
man from sin. God wanted this picture of a sacrificial lamb printed
indelibly in the minds of the people so when Jesus sacrificed his life, they
would know what he was doing and why.

The shedding of blood keeps them aware of the deadliness of sin and
that it is just a temporary fix that doesn't solve the sin problem but merely
delays the day of retribution. Logically, none of this makes sense unless
there'll be a permanent fix that will transform man's unholy sin nature
into a holy nature.

We will look closer at the place of blood in the redemption of man in
the next chapter, but before we do, let us review the biblical story up to
this point. First, there was a history passed down from Adam and Eve.
They had sinned and received the sentence of death. They also received a
promise that God had a plan. All Adam's descendants lived in anticipation
of what that plan would be. When God told Abram to go to a distant land
he didn't know, Abram knew it was beginning. "And in thy seed shall all
the nations of the earth be blessed; because thou hast obeyed my voice"
(Genesis 12:1–2, 22:17–18).

God renewed this promise to Abraham's son, Isaac, and to Isaac's son,

Jacob. God wanted the Israelites to remember who they were and where they came from and to deal with the fact they had nothing to brag about. All their blessings were undeserved gifts from God. They were to remind themselves of that constantly.

> You shall make response before the LORD your God, "A wandering Aramean was my father. And he went down into Egypt and sojourned there, few in number, and there he became a nation, great, mighty, and populous." (Deuteronomy 26:5 ESV)

In setting up the communal life of the new Jewish nation, God combined fasting, celebrating, and sacrifice so together they would keep the people focused on the joy of who they were and how blessed they were and the cost of bringing them to and keeping them in that place of blessing.

As we put this long history in the context of God working to create a holy nation, it begins to make sense. His emphasis on the importance of blood in the forgiveness of sin had been part of a plan for the redemption of the fallen human race. He himself would be the ultimate sacrifice; his blood shed on the altar of sacrifice would set everything right. The logic begins to become clear. The first hint of this plan was given in the Garden of Eden when God foretold what would happen between the woman's seed and the serpent/Satan: "And I will put enmity between thee and the woman, and between thy seed and her seed; it shall bruise thy head, and thou shalt bruise his heel" (Genesis 3:15).

It is not until Paul came on the scene that we are told the rest of God's plan. Paul described the Jewish nation as a tame olive tree and the Gentiles as wild olives being grafted onto the tame olive tree and thereby becoming inheritors of the promises made to Abraham the same as the Jews.

> Know ye therefore that they which are of faith, the same are the children of Abraham. And the scripture, foreseeing that God would justify the heathen through faith, preached before the gospel unto Abraham, saying,

> In thee shall all nations be blessed … And if ye be Christ's,
> then are ye Abraham's seed, and heirs according to the
> promise. (Galatians 3:7–8, 26–29)

While God was doing this, Satan was going through one frustration after another. He didn't know any of this was going to happen. In all his cunning, he didn't foresee it. Satan had lost the ability to understand the power of love. Just when he thought he had it all in the bag, just when he thought the earth would be his staging ground for his next and victorious attack on God's throne, he was forced to make earth the focus of his battle with God.

His slaves on earth had been set free and had been given power and authority over him! His slaves had become his worst enemies.

> Behold! I have given you authority and power to trample
> upon serpents and scorpions, and physical and mental
> strength and ability over all the power that the enemy
> possesses; and nothing shall in any way harm you. (Luke
> 10:19 AMP)

> Verily I say unto you, Whatsoever ye shall bind on earth
> shall be bound in heaven: and whatsoever ye shall loose
> on earth shall be loosed in heaven. (Matthew 18:18 AMP)

> Submit yourselves therefore to God. Resist the devil, and
> he will flee from you. (James 4:7)

These verses are not good news to one whose undisputed might enabled him to assault the throne of God. Nor is it good news to have his whole organization exposed and then have his enemies given God's armor to wear in the fight, armor that was not only for protection but also for attack.

> For we wrestle not against flesh and blood, but against
> principalities, against powers, against the rulers of the
> darkness of this world, against spiritual wickedness in

high places. Wherefore take unto you the whole armour
of God, that ye may be able to with-stand in the evil day,
and having done all, to stand. (Ephesians 6:12–13)

If we accept the conclusion that we have two kingdoms at war with each other, the kingdom of God versus the kingdom Satan is trying to build, the scenario presented is quite logical and plays out as a war strategy. Fasts, ceremonies, and sacrifices were the basic training God put the Hebrews through to prepare them for this war. God carefully works out his plans utilizing the maneuvering of Satan as part of doing his will.

Satan, on the other hand, uses the demons and other fallen angels under his command to entrap people by lust. Yet he is always outmaneuvered and outsmarted as God uses him to help sift the wheat from the chaff, giving everyone the opportunity to decide which kingdom he or she will serve. The Bible does not leave this as a never-ending battle; it all comes to an end. The Bible tells us there is a permanent fix for sin that actually gives us recreated human spirits and removes our sin nature that has held us captive since the Fall. That is the topic of our next chapter, the kinsman-redeemer.

NOTES

CHAPTER 10

Solutions

A man looked across his farm. If the weather held good and prices picked up, he just might be able to stay solvent that year. It was the 1980s in the Midwest. The whole farm economy had suddenly gone berserk as though a bubble had burst. Prices fell. Land that had been overvalued became undervalued. Farmers had to sell their livestock and crops at prices far below what they had paid and were still unable to pay their debts. There was no one to whom they could turn, no one who could redeem their land or pay their debts. Many lost everything. There was no kinsman-redeemer.

That story has been repeated many times over the centuries. It happened in Judea many years ago, but it had a much different ending. A man, his wife, and their two sons stood looking over their farm. The land was parched. Was it the third, fourth, fifth year in a row of drought? It didn't matter. They had spent all their resources hoping the rains would come in time to save their crops. Finally, in desperation, they packed up their possessions and moved to the distant country of Moab. There they settled. They skimped and saved. They dreamed of the day they would have enough saved to redeem their old farm. But alas, that was not to be. The man died.

Meanwhile, the sons had grown up and married Moabite girls. Their widowed mother lived with them; she was destined to spend her remaining years in that far country. That too was not to be for both her sons also died. There was but one thing left she could do. First, set her two daughters-in-law free to return to their families so that in time they could remarry. And then she would return to the place she and her husband had left so many years ago. There at least she had kinsmen from whom she might receive kindnesses now and then.

This woman, whose name was Naomi, was an exceptional woman of character and love. Her daughters-in-law adored her and wanted to remain with her. They would not hear of her leaving without them. Finally, after much persuasion and tears, one daughter-in-law returned to her parents' home. The other was determined to stay with Naomi. The words she spoke at that time continue to echo through the ages: "Whither thou goest, I will go; and where thou lodgest, I will lodge: thy people shall be my people, and thy God my God" (Ruth 1:16).

A Kinsman-Redeemer Ignites Hope

Ruth went with Naomi back to Bethlehem, and Ruth immediately looked for ways to provide for them. One way was to follow the harvesters as they cut the grain. She would pick up the grain that Levitical law required the harvesters to leave behind.[1] From that they could make bread. Ruth asked permission of Naomi to go to the fields.

The field she chose, without knowing it, belonged to Boaz, a relative of Naomi's late husband. Boaz had heard about Naomi and Ruth and was greatly impressed by this young woman's character and her devotion to her mother-in-law. Boaz was a man of honor. He told Ruth he would fulfill the duty of a kinsman-redeemer. He would purchase the land back for Naomi. He would marry Ruth that she might bear a son to be Naomi's heir.

A kinsman-redeemer is far more important than might appear on the surface. It is about a provision God had made in his plan for Israel. God decreed that every Hebrew man should have an inheritance in Israel, his property where he could sit under his own fig tree.[2]

But as so often happens, unexpected situations cause unplanned results. A man could lose his inheritance because of poor choices, or drought, or any number of other reasons. He and his family could become slaves because they had no money to pay their debts. Regardless of what difficulties the intervening years brought, God decreed that every fiftieth year would be a year of jubilee and all would be restored to what it had been in the beginning. Slaves and bondservants were set free, debts were cancelled, and farmland was returned to its original owner. It was a time of beginning again.

Jubilee came only every fifty years. What if you need a jubilee right now? Just as Israel at many different times needed a redeemer for the nation,[3] so too individuals needed redeemers. God made provision for individuals and called it a kinsman-redeemer.[4] Naomi was a widow without a male descendant. She needed more than a redeemer; she needed a son!

Boaz agreed to be Naomi's kinsman-redeemer. He bought back the land that had belonged to Naomi's husband. He married Ruth, and they had a son, who became Naomi's heir. His name was Obed; he became the father of Jesse, the father of David, Israel's greatest king.

There is much more to this story than a romance with a happy ending. The kinsman-redeemer is an important module in God's teaching plan. The people needed to understand the need for the kinsman-redeemer and why this was a key part of his plan. First, it set forth the legal basis of redemption. It made clear that anyone needing redemption could have it if he or she had a kinsman-redeemer. A key requirement was that there had to be a blood connection between the redeemer and the one being redeemed. That blood connection meant that whoever owned the property or the slave was required by law to sell the property or the slave to the kinsman-redeemer at a fair price. He could not legally refuse to sell.

Second, it provided a legal safeguard for the redeemed. A dishonest kinsman could not be a kinsman-redeemer. He could not redeem the property or person only to claim ownership for himself. Because he was a blood kinsman, the law would step in and stop him. By law, when you were redeemed, you were free, and the property was yours free and clear. You didn't owe anyone anything.

The kinsman-redeemer gave immediate relief, but it was not a permanent fix. It was always possible that the problems that had caused the need in the first place could rise up again. God was teaching the people that it was that way with sin. The sacrifice that set them free from Satan for a short time had to be repeated yearly because they kept sinning.

Not only did man need to be redeemed from slavery; his sin nature needed to be transformed so that he wouldn't sin again. Sacrifices at best are nothing more than a temporary escape from Satan's clutches. The tendency and the desire to sin remain.[5] God explained to the Hebrews that there was a limit to how much he could help them. As long as they did their part, as long as they obeyed him and worshiped only him, he could bless them. Otherwise, they would slip out from under his force shield of protection. Only when their sinful nature was transformed would the redemption be permanent.

Needed–A Permanent Fix

The good news is that God has a permanent fix—the kinsman-redeemer. Paul explained the gravity of our situation: "Therefore, as sin came into the world through one man, and death as the result of sin, so death spread to all men, no one being able to stop it or to escape its power because all men sinned" (Romans 5:12 AMP).

The only way out of our sentence of death is to find a kinsman-redeemer who has never sinned and therefore is not a slave of Satan. Only one who is without sin can die in our place and pay the penalty for our sin. Jesus said that was why he had come: "The Son of man came not to be ministered unto, but to minister, and to give his life a ransom for many" (Matthew 20:28).

It's easy to keep falling into sin as we all know. The Hebrews were warned that their rebellion, their sin, took them out from under God's covering and protection. What did they do when their sin got them into trouble? They "remembered" God and came crying, begging God to redeem them. The prophet Isaiah records God's response.

> Fear not, thou worm Jacob, and ye men of Israel; I will
> help thee, saith the LORD, and thy redeemer, the Holy
> One of Israel ... Thus saith the LORD the King of Israel,
> and his redeemer the LORD of hosts; I am the first, and I
> am the last; and beside me there is no God ... Thus saith
> the LORD, thy redeemer, and he that formed thee from
> the womb. (Isaiah 41:14, 44:6, 24)

Man will not be free from Satan's control as long as he has a rebellious sin nature. How is God going to get rid of man's rebellious nature? He can't start over by recreating man; that would be stealing man from Satan, and stealing is logically impossible for God. The law says the sinner must die. Since a man did the sinning, only a man can take a man's place. An animal can't. An angel can't. A man's life must be given.

The Law is plain. The soul that sins must die. Period.[6] A sinless soul could give his life in place of the sinner. It would have to be one who wasn't a slave to Satan. He must also be a kinsman because only a man can die for a man.

But wait! That still doesn't solve the problem. A kinsman-redeemer can die for me only once. After he's dead and I keep on sinning because my nature is sin, I'm back where I started with a death penalty hanging over my head. That means his death didn't do me any good. For it to have done me any good, he needed to take my sin nature to death with him. Only that would set me free. It isn't just my physical body that has to die; my sin nature must also die.

The only way this kinsman-redeemer would work for me is if he literally became me and I became him. He must take my sin nature upon himself while I in turn take his sinless nature upon myself. We trade places. He becomes what I am so I can become what he is. God would not have established fasts, celebrations, sacrifices, and kinsman-redeemers while enduring the fickleness of the Hebrews if that hadn't been his plan and final solution.

The Gift and the Giver

The amazing thing the Bible tells us is that the switch has already been made. A Redeemer has been found. The sacrifice has been made.[7] It was a plan laid down before Adam and Eve were created. The plan was that God's Son, Jesus, our kinsman by birth being born of a woman, would be that sacrifice. It would be God himself taking our place. "For He hath made him to be sin for us, who knew no sin; that we might be made the righteousness of God in him" (2 Corinthians 5:21).

At this point, a couple questions arise that disturb some. The first is, if God was in Christ and Christ died, doesn't that mean God is dead?

The Old Testament, Jesus, and the apostle Paul assert that the Lord our God is one.

> Hear, O Israel: The LORD our God is one LORD. (Deuteronomy 6:4)

> And Jesus answered him, The first of all the commandments is, Hear, O Israel; The Lord our God is one Lord. (Mark 12:29)

> One God and Father of all, who is above all, and through all, and in you all. (Ephesians 4:6)

Jesus said, "I am in the Father, and the Father in me" (John 14:11). He told Philip, "He that hath seen me hath seen the Father; and how sayest thou then, Shew us the Father?" (John 14:9). John stated, "He was in the world, and the world was made by him, and the world knew him not. He came unto his own, and his own received him not" (John 1:10–11). It certainly sounds as though when Jesus died, God died.

The second question is, what does the Bible mean when it tells us that while God is One, he is also God the Father, God the Son, and God the Holy Spirit? This division of God into three persons is seen in the following verses.

> Is not he thy father that hath bought thee? hath he not made thee, and established thee? (Deuteronomy 32:6)

> Thou shalt call me, My father; and shalt not turn away from me. (Jeremiah 3:19)

> The Spirit of God moved upon the face of the waters. (Genesis 1:2)

> And the LORD said, My spirit shall not always strive with man. (Genesis 6:3)

And the Word was made flesh, and dwelt among us, (and we beheld his glory, the glory as of the only begotten of the Father,) full of grace and truth. (John 1:14)

God sent forth his Son, made of a woman. (Galatians 4:4)

He that hath seen me hath seen the Father … Believe me that I am in the Father, and the Father in me. (John 14:9–11)

For in him dwelleth all the fullness of the Godhead bodily. (Colossians 2:9)

How do we reconcile the concept that God is three persons and at the same time one person? As strange as it may seem, we will turn to modern science for the answer. For a long time, dreamers of fantasy wrote about a time machine in which you could travel to the past or to the future. At first, that was just a fantasy of storytellers and science fiction. With the coming of Einstein and the theory of relativity, time travel moved from fantasy to possibility.

To our three-dimensional world, Einstein added time as the fourth dimension. Theoretical physicists have built on this concept and suggest that there may be as many as seven or more dimensions. It wasn't just time travel that suddenly seemed possible. Physicists began to suggest the possibility of multiple dimensions, parallel universes, and alternate realities existing in the same space at the same time. Theorizing about dimensions has enabled physicists to solve many practical problems that were hindering their research.

Given the above, suddenly, the concept of God existing as three in one doesn't seem so illogical. Logic tells us the Creator must be at least as multifaceted and as multidimensional as his creation. It tells us God could send his Son to die our death and raise him to life again.

A Bit of Mind Stretching

The concept of dimensions can be helpful in Bible study. For example, where was the Garden of Eden? There is no archeological evidence of a garden because the garden was not destroyed. If it was not destroyed, where is it? Borrowing from science, we can say that the logical answer is that it is still there but in a dimension we are unable to see: "So he drove out the man; and he placed at the east of the garden of Eden Cherubims, and a flaming sword which turned every way, to keep the way of the tree of life" (Genesis 3:24).

In several places, the Bible suggests the possibility of other dimensions we cannot see. One story concerns the prophet Elisha. The king of Syria was being frustrated in his efforts to capture the king of Israel because Elisha was always telling the king of Israel where to hide. When the king of Syria learned what the prophet Elisha was doing, he sent his army to capture Elisha. On the morning the capture was to take place, the king of Syria had his army surround the city.

> When the servant of the man of God rose early and went out, behold, an army with horses and chariots was around the city. Elisha's servant said to him, Alas, my master! What shall we do? Elisha answered, Fear not; for those with us are more than those with them. Then Elisha prayed, Lord, I pray You, open his eyes that he may see. And the Lord opened the young man's eyes, and he saw, and behold, the mountain was full of horses and chariots of fire round about Elisha. (2 Kings 6:15–17 AMP)

Elisha's servant couldn't see the chariots of the Lord. He could have walked back and forth over every inch of the mountain and not found a trace of them or bumped into any. But once his eyes were opened, once he stepped into that dimension, the chariots of the Lord became visible and real. He could see them; he had been awakened to that dimension. They were solid objects he could bump into. The chariots existed in another dimension and were unseen by the enemy but were able to inflict serious damage on the enemy.

God tells us that he is far greater than our minds can grasp. You and I can be in only one place at one time, but God is in all places at all times!

Do I not fill the heaven and the earth?' declares the Lord. (Jeremiah 23:24 ESV)

For the eyes of the LORD run to and fro throughout the whole earth. (2 Chronicles 16:9)

If I ascend to heaven … If I make my bed in Sheol … If I take the wings of the dawn, if I dwell in the remotest part of the sea, even there Your hand will lead me … If I say, "Surely the darkness will overwhelm me, and the light around me will be night," … the night is as bright as the day. (Psalm 139:7–12 ESV)

"Do I not fill the heavens and the earth?" declares the Lord. (Jeremiah 23:24)

THUS SAYS the Lord: Heaven is My throne, and the earth is My footstool. (Isaiah 66:1 AMP)

The resurrected Jesus gave many examples of his ability to move between dimensions. The disciples were gathered in an upper room, doors closed and locked out of fear. Jesus suddenly appeared in their midst. The first thing he did was prove that he was real. He told them to handle his body. Then he asked for food and ate it. After talking with them, he vanished.[8]

Even Philip stepped into another dimension for a moment. An angel of the lord told him to go on the way that led down from Jerusalem to Gaza. He did and met an Ethiopian eunuch who was reading the prophet Isaiah. Philip led the eunuch to faith in Christ, baptizing him in a pool. Suddenly, the Spirit of the Lord caught Philip away and Philip suddenly found himself in Azotus, some thirty miles away.[9]

As these examples show, we can conclude that God is a multidimensional God. He exists as one God and in three distinct persons—Father, Son, and Holy Spirit.

Do you not believe that I am in the Father, and that the Father is in Me? What I am telling you I do not say on My own authority and of My own accord; but the Father Who lives continually in Me does the (His) works, His own miracles, deeds of power. (John 14:10 AMP)

To this Paul added, "It was God personally present in Christ, reconciling and restoring the world to favor with Himself" (2 Corinthians 5:19 AMP). Though it was through Jesus that all things were created and in him that all things are held together,[10] it was Jesus who said, "Go to My brethren and tell them, I am ascending to My Father and your Father, and to My God and your God" (John 20:17).

God Who Made Us Redeems Us

With the above in mind, we follow the unfolding story of the Redeemer who gave his life as a ransom for us. The apostle John wrote that the Word was in the beginning with God and the Word was God, that without the Word was not anything made that was made, and that the Word became flesh, Jesus, and dwelt among us.[11] Turning back to Genesis, we read that God's Spirit moved on the face of the waters when he made the earth: "And the earth was without form, and void; and darkness was upon the face of the deep. And the Spirit of God moved upon the face of the waters" (Genesis 1:2).

We are introduced to God's Son in Proverbs 8. The Son was always with God and was God's delight. The Son is called the Wisdom of God, the Builder and the Glue.

The LORD possessed me in the beginning of his way, before his works of old. I was set up from ever- lasting, from the beginning, or ever the earth was ... Then I was by him, as one brought up with him: and I was daily his delight, rejoicing always before him. (Proverbs 8:22–31)

For it was in Him that all things were created, in heaven and on earth, things seen and things unseen, whether

> thrones, dominions, rulers, or authorities; all things were created and exist through Him by His service, intervention and in and for Him. And He Himself existed before all things, and in Him all things consist (cohere, are held together). (Colossians 1:16–17 AMP)

God made plans for our redemption before he made Adam and Eve. Why was our redemption so important to him? While we cannot know God's mind, it is enough to know that God's heart is love. He shows that love in his plan to be our Redeemer. God will be in his Son as the one who was without sin. His sacrificial death will atone for humanity's sins.

But wait! God is God, not man. Doesn't the Redeemer have to be a sinless man? Yes. How can God be a man? That was God's secret plan. His Son would divest himself of all it meant to be God and submit himself to be born of a woman: "But when the fullness of the time was come, God sent forth his Son, made of a woman, made under the law, to redeem them that were under the law, that we might receive the adoption of sons" (Galatians 4:4–5).

> Who, being in the form of God, thought it not robbery to be equal with God: But made himself of no reputation, and took upon him the form of a servant, and was made in the likeness of men: And being found in fashion as a man, he humbled himself, and became obedient unto death, even the death of the cross. (Philippians 2:6–9)

If Jesus was born of a woman, wasn't he born with a sin nature? No! The sin nature is passed down from the male, not the female. We are told that Eve was deceived but that Adam had sinned. The female may have a sin nature, but she doesn't pass it on to her progeny; they get it from their father. Why didn't Jesus sin like the rest of us? He did not have an earthly father; it wasn't in his nature to sin!

Some men live and breathe hunting and fishing; it's in their nature; some would say it's in their blood. But an ad for a fishing rod and reel that would set a fisherman's mouth watering is what I would wrap garbage in; it holds no attraction for me. I have no interest in firearms either; it's not in my nature.

Because Jesus didn't have a sin nature, sin held no attraction for him. For him to sin, he would have had to have done so deliberately; he would have had to have made a conscious effort to do what was not natural for him. Adam on the other hand gave in to the temptation to be like God. The child Jesus had nothing to gain; Satan knew that. But there would come a time when Jesus had much to gain. That is why Satan waited to strike until Jesus came of age and was setting out on his life's mission. Satan could then offer Jesus what only Satan had the authority to give.

Satan acknowledged who Jesus was—the Son of God. He acknowledged that Jesus was on a mission with a purpose that would cost Jesus untold suffering and anguish and even his life. Satan reminded Jesus that as the one through whom all things were created, he had the power to turn stones into bread.[12] He had the power and authority to flood the scribes and Pharisees and the Roman army with mind-blowing signs and wonders and destroy them if he wanted to. At one point, Jesus said, "Do you imagine that I could not appeal to my Father, and he would at once send more than twelve legions of angels to defend me?" (Matthew 26:53 PHP).

The temptation Satan offered Jesus was to give him on a silver platter everything God had promised, the kingdoms of this world, without his having to suffer and be crucified. Each temptation with which Satan tempted Jesus was designed to seduce Jesus to gain what he wanted by joining the rebellion.[13] Jesus chose to obey God and trust him to do what he had promised. "Who for the joy that was set before him endured the cross, despising the shame, and is set down at the right hand of the throne of God" (Hebrews 12:2).

What do we conclude from all we've considered in this chapter? Our study has brought us to the point that we find the Bible's story coming together in the person of a kinsman-redeemer by whose death and resurrection the way has been opened for us to return to that place of glory and power and brilliance man once knew before the Fall. The one who has made this possible, we are told, is our kinsman-redeemer, our Father and our brother, Jesus.

NOTES

CHAPTER 11

The Missing Piece

Have you ever had the feeling of confusion that comes from being left in the dark about something that everyone else seems to know about and nobody is telling you? Have you experienced the frustration of trying to put together a puzzle when some pieces are missing? By its nature, the Bible can leave us feeling that a piece is missing, that there's something else we need to know. When we ask experts for answers, they only add to our confusion because of all their different ideas, opinions, and beliefs.

If God did create the heavens and the earth as the Bible claims, why? Why was the universe created? Why were you and I created? Evolution tries to get around these questions by saying it just happened, but that doesn't answer the question of where it all came from. The Bible presents us with an elaborate history. It explains that the creation of the universe was intentional and that our creation was even more intentional. Why? What motivated God? That's the unanswered question, the missing piece. What motivates God? Why did God do it? What does the Bible say?

Looking Down from the Mountaintop

The view from the top of Pike's Peak in Colorado is worth the trip up. On the way up, you have no idea what awaits you. You are focused on negotiating narrow roads and hairpin curves. But when you reach the top, the view is absolutely amazing! You look down and the whole scene is laid out before you. On the left, you see the road you traveled come into view. Your eyes sweep along the road to towns you've driven through, places where you've taken wrong turns, places where you got lost, and places where you stopped. At your far right, the road vanishes into the distance. The whole valley is laid out before you in one grand mosaic. Up there, it is easy to see your path, but down there, it was easy to get lost!

Perhaps this analogy will help us see the Bible more clearly. The Bible is the valley we see stretched out before us. The mountaintop is a vantage point outside time and space from which we can look down upon the panoramic view of the biblical story. On our far left we see creation begin. It's a marvelous sight. Stars and planets burst into being much like fireworks, except these stars and planets seem to be alive in some strange way for they are singing the glory of God (Job 38:7).

Next, God creates a multitude of intelligent beings, some of whom we recognize as angels. They possess what we call a will, for they are expected to make intelligent and creative choices when carrying out their tasks. But it also means they have the freedom to disobey God. One being stands out—the archangel Lucifer, who appears to be the most outstanding, beautiful, and talented of all the angelic beings God created. All we see up to this point is very good because God is good. Good can create only good.

When our eyes move a little to the right, we become aware of a darkness that seems to be growing in Lucifer. The darkness spreads from Lucifer to other beings. Then suddenly, Lucifer attacks the throne of God and there is war in the heavens. Lucifer and his hosts are defeated. One planet is left in utter chaos. Most of Lucifer's angel army is bound in prison. Time passes. The dark planet is recreated, turned into a beautiful garden. From the soil, God creates two beings who are like him. He gives them the earth. But Lucifer, now Satan, uses a diabolical plan to trick man into giving the earth back to him. Man, who was once king, is reduced to a slave under Satan's dominion. At this point, God begins to unfold a plan he had put in place before he created the world.

As our eyes continue moving to the right, we see evil grow until one day God picks Noah and his family to escape a flood that comes and drowns all living things. All that has happened up to that point is prehistory. Geological evidence shows that there was a flood. Geological and archeological evidence of the existence of man prior to the flood seems to be missing. Apart from the list of people groups that spread out after the flood, the biblical narrative picks up with Abraham.

As our eyes continue to follow the biblical narrative, we note that it records men talking with God. This is especially so when it comes to Abraham, who hears God speak and goes where God sends him. Abraham's trust in God was so great he knew that when God told him to sacrifice Isaac, if God did not provide a sacrificial substitute, God would raise Isaac from the dead.[1] This is followed by a long panoramic stretch in which Abraham's descendants, a stubborn and rebellious people, are taught and prepared to fulfill God's plan.

Directly in front of us in this panoramic view of the biblical narrative, we see something strange as though history was beginning to work backwards. We see God come as his Son. He comes untainted by sin, having no earthly father to pass the sin genes on to him. He faces all the temptations that led to the Fall but doesn't sin. Being without sin, he is able to and does take upon himself the sins of all men past, present, and future and pay the penalty of death for all men. He became sin for us that we might become the righteousness of God.[2] By killing Jesus, Satan set us free from the law of sin and death: "For the law of the Spirit of life in Christ Jesus hath made me free from the law of sin and death" (Romans 8:2). Then God raised us up together with Jesus so that Jesus has become the firstborn among many brethren.[3]

History continues to work backward as we are given instructions on how to live as overcomers, bringing to naught all Satan's efforts to steal, kill, and destroy. Finally, we witness the ultimate demise of Satan and his followers. The redeemed receive a glorious and undreamed of future.

Again we ask why? What motivates God? From our vantage point, a possible answer seems to emerge. One word seems to rise up. It may not catch your attention at first, but it is there throughout the panoramic view. The word is both familiar and unfamiliar—familiar because we use it all the time, unfamiliar because when used of God, its meaning is transformed. That word is *grace*.

We first hear of grace in Genesis 6:8 where it is written, "Noah found grace in the eyes of the Lord." What is this grace that Noah found? When we dig into the meaning of the word *grace*, when it's speaking about God, we discover that it means unceasing goodwill, unlimited forgiveness, and unconditional love. That's what Noah found. It was given him as a gift unasked for and undeserved.

Logically, as we concluded earlier, God's nature is love. Sin is a destroyer whose's nature is to curse, demand and inflict punishment. It is God's nature to bless; he finds pleasure in that. We are told that we are a delight to him and he enjoys our company. It is his nature to think good of and for us.[4] At first, we wonder if that is really true. Doesn't the Bible teach that God punishes sinners? When we examine the Bible closely, we find man punishes himself; when he doesn't abide under the shadow of the Almighty (Psalm 91), he is out from under his protection. God shows us his lovingkindness and favor, but it is up to us to receive it or reject it. That is grace.

God's eagerness to bless was explained by Jesus in his Sermon on the Mount.

> Or what man is there of you, whom if his son ask bread, will he give him a stone? Or if he ask a fish, will he give him a serpent? If ye then, being evil, know how to give good gifts unto your children, how much more shall your Father which is in heaven give good things to them that ask him? (Matthew 7:9–11)

John explained that God's motivation was grace. It is because God forgives with unlimited forgiveness and loves with unconditional love that he took our place so we would not have to perish.[5] Because he loves, Jesus came. Because he loves, it's his pleasure to give good things to those who ask him. By grace, Jesus took our sin nature upon himself and gave us his sinless nature. Every time his grace is accepted, he dances for joy.[6] That is grace.

Grace cannot be measured, weighed, bottled, or sold; it can only be experienced. The examples that follow illustrate God's grace in action. You can easily give other explanations for what happened, but if you're honest and logical, you'll admit that it can just as easily be said that these are incidences of God's grace.

Transforming Grace

The hardened heart melts in the presence of grace. That's what happened in this true story about a man and his son. Fred (not his real name) was highly esteemed in his church and community, but he carried a great burden in his heart. His estranged son, who he hadn't seen in several years, was heavily involved in drugs—using and selling. Unable to bear the anguish any longer, Fred went to see Hegge Iverson, the founder of Burden Bearers.

Fred went through his long list of grievances. Hegge stopped him. "You aren't telling me facts about your son. You're cursing him!" That statement shocked Fred. When asked what he meant, Hegge instructed Fred to replace each grievance with a blessing, with the truth of God's Word and the power of God's love. Light replaces darkness. Righteousness overcomes unrighteousness.

Fred and his wife's words and attitudes about their son radically changed. When they spoke of him after that, they blessed him instead of cursing him. The day came when Hegge instructed them to begin thanking God for bringing their son home. Hegge told Fred that when his son came home, he was to take him to the finest restaurant and have them prepare his son's favorite dinner.

Several weeks later, the son came home. They greeted him with open arms and told him they had been expecting him. Then Fred said, "I'm taking you to dinner." The son, already confused by this display of acceptance and love, protested that his clothes were dirty and he hadn't washed his hair in months. "You look just fine to us," they said, "just the way you are."

Fred had thought and spoken blessings toward his son for so long that he was genuinely overjoyed to see him. He really did like him just the way he was just as God likes us just the way we are.[7] The son couldn't believe what he was hearing. Not one negative thing was said. No questions about drugs. The son was bewildered. That night, Fred asked forgiveness for failing him as a father. And that night, his son experienced unlimited forgiveness, unconditional love. His father had learned to love as God loves. The son, expecting to receive criticism and disapproval, received grace instead, and his heart melted. Surrounded by unlimited forgiveness and unconditional love, he changed completely and now pastors a church in the Midwest. That is the power of God's grace. It isn't earned, deserved, or bought; it is freely given because that is what love does. "If God be for us, who can be against us?" (Romans 8:31).

Are you willing to allow the logical possibility that the change came about because his parents graced him with God's grace?

Healing Grace

Dr. Bill Reed, MD, believes all healing comes from God's grace. It is God who heals; doctors only assist. Dr. Reed teaches that to help a patient, the doctor must take time to love the patient with the God kind of love.[8] The doctor must always be open to the leading of the Holy Spirit at any time and in any place. He tells the following story to illustrate.

He was in a restaurant meeting with the board of directors of his Christian Medical Foundation. A woman had collapsed just as she was leaving the restaurant. Another doctor had pronounced her dead. Dr. Reed felt a prompting in his spirit to go to the woman. He spoke to the husband. "Sir, it looks like you've lost your wife, but let me try something." He prayed for the woman. He hit her chest using a technique he knew. She gasped and came back to life. An ambulance took her to the hospital.

About an hour and a half later, a man came into the restaurant looking for Dr. Reed. He said tests were given and his wife had been pronounced okay. She was in the car. God's grace flowing through Dr. Reed loving a woman who needed to experience grace, made the difference. Grace had enabled Dr. Reed to tune in to the woman and to God. Grace gave life. "If God be for us, who can be against us?" (Romans 8:31).

According to Dr. Reed, doctors are one aspect of God's grace we all experience. When the doctor is tuned in to God and tuned in to the patient, he becomes a channel for God to pour out his grace.

Everyday Grace

We are often blind to the gifts God's grace pours on us. We don't recognize them as gifts of grace. Instead, we give credit to other things or people.

At first, I thought what happened to me one day was unusual, but then I rationalized a reason for it.

When I was nearing graduation from high school, we went to visit my dad's cousin, Christine, and her husband, Milton. I liked Milton and Christine, and I especially liked the fact that they had a sailboat with kitchen and bunks! As much as I wanted to go sailing with them, it never worked out. One day, Milton said, "If you can't go to college because you can't afford it, we want to pay your way."

Christine and Milton were childless. I had done nothing to deserve their offer. I assumed they were seeing in me the son they had never had. Later, I realized their offer was undeserved grace. God was telling me He would see to it that could afford go to college. Which was to say that I did not have any excuse for not going. Many times, the blessings we enjoy we attribute to other things such as luck, or the generosity of others, or even chance. But all blessings come from God who delights in blessing us.

Something happens that can be explained only by attributing it to God's grace. Too many things all come together at just the right time in the right places and in perfect sequence. In 1955, my army buddy Ferris and I attended an armed services religious retreat at a beautiful mountain setting in Germany. One of the chaplains there told wonderful stories of his adventures in Jerusalem—rafting on the Jordan River and swimming in the Dead Sea.

As he talked, the desire to visit the Holy Land began to burn in us. We had no money, so it would happen only if God worked out the finances. He would have to give us the trip and prepare a way for us where there was no way.[9] We were two young soldiers who had the audacity to believe God's unmerited grace was meant for us.

We asked but received no answer. We decided to act as though God had said yes. We filled out all the paperwork and got all the immunizations. Still no word from God. Since the only way we could afford to go was to hitch rides on air force planes, we headed for the air force base at Wiesbaden, Germany. No planes were going to North Africa or Egypt, the direction we needed to go. After waiting and praying all day we decided to take the first plane out that was going to England.

It was the next morning at the servicemen's hotel in London that we got our answer. There on the bulletin board was a notice of a plane going to North Africa. When we saw that sign, we knew by an overwhelming inner witness that God had given us our trip. Strange wasn't it that we had to go north to go south? We flew over 5,558 miles; at each step of the way, God sent people to travel with us and guide us.

At the Cairo airport, the director of business and finance for the University of Maryland introduced himself to us. He too was going to Jerusalem. He showed us how to see more and do more for far less money than we would have known to do. God knew we needed all the help we could get. The same thing happened when we stepped out of our taxi in Beirut. A hotel owner had his car stop just as we stepped foot on the sidewalk. He gave us rooms and meals for very little cost and introduced us to the pilots of an air force executive plant that would take us back to Europe the next day.

The total cost of this amazing journey was less than $150 apiece! God gave us an amazing journey. He looked after us when we didn't know enough to look after ourselves. The journey and God's care of us was a totally undeserved gift of grace. Grace means that it is the Father's good pleasure to give us good things.[10]

Motivating Grace

God embraces us with unlimited forgiveness and unconditional love. Our society's motto is, "Do the crime, do the time." We think in terms of wrath and judgment, of getting even, of making others pay for what they did. We don't love all people because all people aren't lovable. Even within our families, it's often difficult to give unlimited forgiveness to say nothing of unconditional love.

Grace is an everyday word we don't think much about. Grace is a host doing more than is required. The time after something is due before a penalty is imposed is called a grace period. "Gracious me!" is used to express surprise. This is not what the Bible means when it speaks of God's grace.

In Hebrew, "grace" is used to describe God's actions toward us. It's a heartfelt response by God to our desperate need for a redeemer and his heartfelt desire to bless us with every good thing. There is a sense in which God takes pleasure in fixing things we can't fix. For instance, five armies were arrayed against Judah and King Jehoshaphat threatening to destroy them,[11] but by his grace, God fixed it.

There was the widow of Zarephath who with her son was about to die of starvation. Because of a drought, there was no food or oil to be had. God blessed her with a barrel of meal and oil that wouldn't fail.[12] It is suggested that God cries when we cry.[13] God sits in jovial anticipation as we unwrap an undeserved gift such as unexpected money to pay an overdue bill or to take a vacation. God's grace is God's heartfelt response to our desperate needs as well as our desires. Heartfelt means from the heart. John explains God's grace this way.

> For out of His fullness (abundance) we have all received, all had a share, and we were all supplied with one grace after another and spiritual blessing upon spiritual blessing and even favor upon favor and gift heaped upon gift. (John 1:16 AMP)

The unmerited and undeserved grace of God is his nature. It is who he is. Wrath gives him no pleasure. God doesn't take pleasure in the death of anyone.[14] We see his grace in the over 7,487 promises of blessings he has for us! He takes pleasure in bestowing grace on those who look to him. As Paul wrote, "And God is able to make all grace abound toward you; that ye, always having all sufficiency in all things, may abound to every good work" (2 Corinthians 9:8).

His heart grieves over those who refuse his grace.

> O Jerusalem, Jerusalem, thou that killest the prophets, and stonest them which are sent unto thee, how often would I have gathered thy children together, even as a hen gathereth her chickens under her wings, and ye would not! (Matthew 23:37)

We sing "Amazing Grace" for that is what it is. Paul wrote,

> But God, who is rich in mercy, for his great love wherewith he loved us, Even when we were dead in sins,

hath quickened us together with Christ, (by grace ye are saved;) And hath raised us up together, and made us sit together in heavenly places in Christ Jesus: That in the ages to come he might shew the exceeding riches of his grace in his kindness toward us through Christ Jesus. For by grace are ye saved through faith; and that not of yourselves: it is the gift of God: Not of works, lest any man should boast. (Ephesians 2:4–8)

God lavished his grace on his chosen people. He knew exactly what they were like.[15] God used their defects to demonstrate to the world the greatness of his grace. Israel was the tame olive, and we were the wild olive that was grafted onto the tame olive, and by that, we too became the seed of Abraham and heirs of his blessing.[16]

In the fullness of time, Israel will fulfill the purpose for which God called it into being and gave it a land. Ezekiel and Daniel contain many references that tell what is happening to Israel today and is about to happen in the near future.[17] When we fit this into the view from the top of the mountain, it is a picture of amazing grace!

The Bible declares that there is purpose and hope for everyone who has lived.[18] All people from all ages and all times will stand before him at the Great White Throne Judgment. Grace will be there so everyone will have one last opportunity to choose Jesus and live.

And I saw a great white throne, and him that sat on it, from whose face the earth and the heaven fled away; and there was found no place for them. And I saw the dead, small and great, stand before God; and the books were opened: and another book was opened, which is the book of life: and the dead were judged out of those things which were written in the books, according to their works. (Revelation 20:11–15)

He that heareth my word, and believeth on him that sent me, hath everlasting life, and shall not come into condemnation; but is passed from death unto life. (John 5:24)

The Christian has nothing to fear for grace has washed him clean of all sin by the blood of Jesus. One's lot in life may be unfair, but it is only for a duration.[19] The Bible tells us that if we study the scriptures and learn about and use the tools God has provided for our use, our situations will change dramatically. Satan tries to brainwash us and keep us ignorant, weak, and unbelieving. He floods our minds with doubts, church traditions, and doctrines full of errors. God tells us to use our heads, believe what he has written, and act on it. The truth will set us free.[20]

NOTES

CHAPTER 12

It's Time for an Honest Answer

Do you always believe what someone else tells you to believe? Especially if they belittle you for not believing it? Do you accept the cliché that's worked its way into our culture: "Fifty million Frenchmen can't be wrong" when in truth they often are? Especially when the words were originally used to justify a questionable lifestyle? Do you follow the masses like lemmings plunging over the cliff?

Or do you search for the truth? Do you look for the things others are not telling you? Do you question opinions and prejudices to see if they are based on fact? These are tough questions. They are made tougher by a common pitfall into which we all fall. Jesus gave us a warning about this that is generally ignored. It is ignored because he tells us not to fall into that pitfall. This is his statement.

> But love ye your enemies, and do good, and lend, hoping for nothing again; and your reward shall be great, and ye shall be the children of the Highest: for he is kind unto the unthankful and to the evil. Be ye therefore merciful, as your Father also is merciful. Judge not, and ye shall not be judged: condemn not, and ye shall not be condemned: forgive, and ye shall be forgiven: (Luke 6:35–37)

Judging is the cause of many of our problems. We are misjudged and we misjudge others and what they say. We let another person's opinion spoil our enjoyment of a movie or a book or keep us from a restaurant we would have enjoyed. We let our opinions and beliefs be formed by those who are supposed to be experts instead of searching for the truth ourselves.

The Bible does not give us the option of being its judge because judgment is not what it's about. Many people think it is and gladly join in spreading condemnation around. That's one of the reasons we have trouble with the Bible. Reading it can make us uncomfortable if we find our minds flooded with thoughts of condemnation. We are wrong to read it that way, to read it subjectively instead of objectively. We don't like it when others presume to judge us by quoting it. They are wrong to do that. Jesus stated very clearly that he did not come to condemn the world but to enable all of us to pass from death into life.[1]

Nowhere does it suggest that we must become perfect, give up certain things, change in certain ways, or do certain things. Don't let anyone tell you differently; they can't find scriptures to prove it. All the Bible requires is that we accept God's gift of life with no strings attached, no preconditions we must fulfill. Charlotte Elliott caught this truth in her song.

> Just as I am, without one plea,
> but that thy blood was shed for me,
> and that thou bidst me come to thee,
> O Lamb of God, I come, I come.
> (Charlotte Elliott, 1789–1871)

If God wants us to change, he'll do the changing. That's his responsibility after we accept his gift of grace.

> And I am convinced and sure of this very thing, that He
> Who began a good work in you will continue until the
> day of Jesus Christ (right up to the time of His return),
> developing (that good work) and perfecting and bringing
> it to full completion in you. (Philippians 1:6 AMP)

The Parable of One Thousand Parts

When a child, I loved to read *Popular Mechanics* because it stirred my imagination. Once, it showed me how to build a gyrocopter and fly it wherever I wanted. All I needed were a few tools and a lot of money. The tools I could borrow from my dad. The money I never could earn or borrow. I really wanted to build that gyrocopter. I used to picture myself flying around, landing wherever I wanted, and having a great time. That was my dream. It's still there in the back of my mind.

As I grew older, I never stopped dreaming. One day, I stumbled onto something else. It wasn't a gyrocopter, but it was something I could afford to build. I bought a kit to build a television set. That was back in the days of black and white television. There were no printed circuits and transistors. I had to solder resistors and capacitors onto circuit boards and fit receiving tubes into their sockets. When I first opened the packing box, I was almost overwhelmed by the hundreds of parts. But lying on top of it all was the most important book you could imagine: step-by-step assembly instructions!

Just like it said to do, I got cupcake pans and sorted the hundreds of parts. The instructions said to always double-check the parts and the values printed on them. If I mixed up the parts, the TV wouldn't work. Detailed instructions showed me how to solder so all my connections would be just right. Finally, the day came when the last connection had been soldered and the last screw tightened. The moment of truth.

I gingerly plugged the power cord into the wall socket. So far so good—no puff of smoke, no explosion. Then I turned the power on. Slowly, all the tubes heated up to their operating temperatures and the picture tube came alive with the familiar snow picture and static coming from the speakers. I turned the tuner to a local television station while I held my breath. The picture tube filled with a real picture and the familiar sounds of the program burst forth from the speakers. Ah! The exhilaration of success!

That step-by-step instruction book without which I couldn't have built the TV is similar to the Bible. In addition to detailed instructions to follow, it also had in the back a large section devoted to troubleshooting. These were instructions telling what to do to fix anything that could have gone wrong in building the TV. Success was guaranteed! The Bible also claims that it too is filled with troubleshooting guides.

The Bible forces us to face a dilemma. What will we do with the Bible? Are we willing to take a chance and trust it? When I saw the construction manual for the TV, I had to decide to trust that it wouldn't lead me wrong and that when I made mistakes, it would tell me how to correct them. Am I willing to trust the Bible that much? It does no good to argue that the two books are different. The proof is in the doing, not the debating.

Paul argued that we should give the Bible at least that much consideration.[2] In his letter to Timothy, he wrote, "All scripture is given by inspiration of God, and is profitable for doctrine, for reproof, for correction, for instruction in righteousness: That the man of God may be perfect, throughly furnished unto all good works" (2 Timothy 3:16–17). The apostle Peter agreed with Paul: "Knowing this first, that no prophecy of the scripture is of any private interpretation. For the prophecy came not in old time by the will of man: but holy men of God spake as they were moved by the Holy Ghost" (2 Peter 1:20–21).

The Parable of the Wildflowers

The building had collapsed. The home in which I grew up had stood empty for many years and had been looted. The bedroom where I used to sleep was just a pile of boards with bits of airplane-covered wallpaper sticking up here and there. The old tree where I had a tree house lay on the ground, a fallen victim of wind and storm. It could be said that all that was left of my childhood home was memories, but that wasn't true. My childhood home was more than a house. It was also fields and woods through which I wandered and discovered secrets. Deep in those woods, the wildflowers grew. Underneath the field grass where I had to search for them, the most delicious tasting strawberries grew.

I had to go looking for the wildflowers if I wanted to see them. Looking was rewarded with displays of beauty that took the breath away: The white jack-in-the-pulpit, standing in his green pulpit, sticking his head up through the snow, boldly announcing that winter is over and spring is here. The tiny, three-petal red trillium, the bright-white sunbursts of bloodroots, and the pale white and yellow puffs of Dutchman's breeches graced the floor of the woodland and decorated the edges of little streams.

If I searched diligently in the fields, carefully pushing the grass away, I found wild strawberries with a flavor no store-bought berries could ever match. In their season, wild raspberries and blackberries were waiting for me to find them. I had to look and push my way through tall grass and underbrush. There were no big signs pointing down saying "Here." The berries were big, hanging over the edges of the creek. I had to wear long-sleeved shirts because the briars were extra sharp, but the flavor of the berries was wonderfully delicious.

Could it be possible that hidden in the midst of brush and thorns we do not understand, buried in the moss and leaves of things on the woodland floor that seem to contradict what we do know, that the Bible holds treasures of inestimable value and joy? You and I are faced with a dilemma—what will we do with the Bible? There is no way to know except as the psalmist wrote: "O taste and see that the LORD is good: blessed is the man that trusteth in him" (Psalm 34:8).

In many ways, the New Testament is a place where wildflowers grow. We must search to find its treasures and its wisdom. When we do, we are richly rewarded. When you study the Bible, you may reach conclusions different from mine or those of another. But that is okay if we reached them honestly and logically as the Bible demands. Believing as I do is not important. "Christ in you the hope of glory," is what's important.[3]

Wonder-Working Power

In the book of Acts, we read how the church was born as thousands received the Good News, repented, and received Jesus as their Lord and Savior. It wasn't the teaching they heard or the inflamed speech of an orator whipping them up into an emotional frenzy that caused them to repent and receive Jesus. It was the manifested miracle working power of God as Peter said quite plainly: "Ye men of Israel, why marvel ye at this? or why look ye so earnestly on us, as though by our own power or holiness we had made this man to walk?" (Acts 3:12).

When asked, "By what power, or by what name, have ye done this?" Peter answered, "Be it known unto you all, and to all the people of Israel, that by the name of Jesus Christ of Nazareth, whom ye crucified, whom God raised from the dead, even by him doth this man stand here before you whole" (Acts 4:10).

Luke summed up what was happening: "And with great power gave the apostles witness of the resurrection" (Acts 4:33). Paul also made it clear that talk and emotions had nothing to do with it.

> And my speech and my preaching was not with enticing words of man's wisdom, but in demonstration of the Spirit and of power ...That your faith should not stand in the wisdom of men, but in the power of God. For the kingdom of God is not in word, but in power. (1 Corinthians 2:4, 5, 4:20)

It was the miracle-working power of God that convinced the people beyond any shadow of doubt that the message they heard was true especially when the man they were talking about in whose name was wonder-working power had been crucified and then rose from the dead only a short time before.

> They brought forth the sick into the streets, and laid them on beds and couches, that at the least the shadow of Peter passing by might overshadow some of them. There came also a multitude out of the cities round about unto Jerusalem, bringing sick folks, and them which were vexed with unclean spirits: and they were healed every one. (Acts 5:15–16)

The historical record bears witness to these events. Those who do not want to believe in the face of all the accepted criteria for judging historical documents will deny the truth of the historical documents. Which side do you choose to be on?

Wildflowers in Unlikely Places

Are churches unlikely places to find wildflowers growing? According to Paul, some are. He said things could get pretty raunchy in some churches. He reminded them that their bodies were members of Christ. But they had made themselves members of a harlot. He told them to stop messing around, stop tricking each other.[4]

From the beginning, churches have been messes on the way to getting cleaned up. And why not? They are made up of people just like you and me. That is why we have to search to find the wildflowers. In every church, we'll find ordinary people with remarkable stories to share. Perhaps a Dr. Richard Eby.

The man who stood in front of us was of slender build and average height. His dark, wavy hair was combed back, and eyes sparkled through his glasses. He was an osteopathic physician specializing in obstetrics and gynecology. He told an amazing story. He was in Chicago helping his wife get the old family mansion ready to sell. He had just taken a heavy box of debris to a second-floor balcony to throw to the paving below. As he leaned forward to drop the box, the old railing gave way. He fell head-first onto the concrete.

Dr. Eby's skull was split open. All the blood drained out of his body. Everything about him spelled death. But death was not to be. Through the prayers of his wife and many others, life came back into him. That in itself was a miracle. But there was more to his story. His spirit left his body the instant his head hit the concrete. One moment he was in suburban Chicago, and the next moment he was in the most exquisite place.

He was thrilled by the sight of Paradise—forests perfect in every detail, the valley floor gorgeous with stately grasses and flowers. He heard beautiful, melodious, angelic music. He smelled a perfume so exotic, refreshing, and superior, that it was fit only for a king.[5] He began to understand what Paul meant when he said that no eye has seen nor ear heard what God has prepared for those who love Him.[6]

Did Dr. Eby actually experience a glimpse of heaven? If you choose, you can quote experts who will give you many alternative explanations for his vision. Dr. Eby believed he did. For that reason, he diligently researched the Bible and found scriptures that verified all he had seen. He brought back no samples we could examine. We can only assume that it happened just as he described. He had nothing to gain from making it up. Because he had established an outstanding reputation as a physician and surgeon, he had much to lose if he was labeled a quack.

A Glorious Company of Warts and Thorns

Jesus graciously and lovingly accepts us just the way we are warts and all. Look at the difficulties he had with the twelve he chose to be with him. One denied him. Others argued about who would have first place when Jesus was king. One was a doubter. One betrayed him. None understood him. One tried to kill all his followers.

None of us is perfect; we are all flawed. Paul refers to new Christian as babies that begin on milk and progress to solid food.

> I, brethren, could not speak unto you as unto spiritual, but as unto carnal, even as babes in Christ … I have fed you with milk, and not with meat … For ye are yet carnal: for whereas there is among you envying, and strife, and divisions, are ye not carnal, and walk as men? (1 Corinthians 3:1–3)

In any gathering of people, you will always find evil present in some form. It may be expressed in selfishness, greed, lack of concern for others, a me-first attitude, a know-it-all attitude, feelings easily hurt, etc. You could attribute these to human nature. The point is that human nature is flawed. Don't let the flaws you see, the thorns on the berry bushes, keep you from enjoying the good berries. The Bible teaches that the thorns are Satan at work trying to distract us and steal our joy, trying to put sickness, poverty, and death upon us. Jesus said, "The thief cometh not, but for to steal, and to kill, and to destroy: I am come that they might have life, and that they might have it more abundantly" (John 10:10).

The evidence tells us that Satan has invaded local churches and denominations to exploit our weaknesses. But God's grace, his undeserved love and favor, accepts us just as we are and forgives us of our sins 24/7 when we ask.[7] Once we understand that, we are ready to look at the church as a place where the wildflowers also grow. You will have to look for them. When you find them, you will be rewarded with delightful beauty and fragrance.

We will find the greatest benefit if we find a local church where we are comfortable and accepted just as we are and where we are willing to accept those people just as they are. It is easier to grow and mature in following Christ and becoming conformed to his likeness when we do it together rather than separately.[8] As it says in Proverbs 27:17 (ESV), "Iron sharpens iron, and one man sharpens another."

If Our Lives Have Purpose, Where Does It Lead?

The book of Revelation contains a description of what will happen in the future. Chapter 20 tells us that Satan will be bound for a thousand years in the bottomless pit. During this time, Jesus will reign on earth. What will it be like? Imagine a time of peace and plenty around the world. No more starvation. No more despots wreaking havoc on innocent people and children. No more disease. No more threats of war. No more terrorism. Everyone will be enjoying the riches of the land and of technology.

Imagine being able to work and live without frustration. Imagine all the people of the world having enough to meet all their needs and to fulfill all their desires. Imagine living in a world without crime and war. Imagine all people united into one family of brothers and sisters who live together in harmony.

It will happen as we become more and more conformed to the image of Jesus. As Paul wrote, "For whom he did foreknow, he also did predestinate to be conformed to the image of his Son, that he might be the firstborn among many brethren" (Romans 8:29).

When you consider the diversity of people and cultures, blending them into one beautiful and harmonious mosaic will not be easy. It will take thousands of thousands of teachers and miracles beyond count to bring the message of love to those who know it not.

Imagine what it will be like when it happens. Imagine having the time to learn all the things you want to learn. Imagine not having to worry about money. Imagine weather that is always ideal. Imagine the tremendous leaps technology will take. Imagine people finally getting their personal lives straightened out. Imagine the hostile areas of the earth flourishing with vegetation. It will be a place where the wildflowers grow.

You can believe what can't be believed by being willing to set aside your prejudices, opinions, and beliefs for which you have no provable evidence and accepting the possibility that it could be, that it could have happened as the Bible said it did, remembering, "For the invisible things of him from the creation of the world are clearly seen, being understood by the things that are made, even his eternal power and Godhead" (Romans 1:20 AMP).

Are you up to the challenge?

NOTES

Endnotes

Introduction: The Star Car

[1]   Psalm 19:1, 97:6; Romans 1:18–23.

Chapter 1: The Incredible Story

[1]   Exodus 3:14.
[2]   Hebrews 11:3; 2 Peter 3:5.
[3]   1 Kings 8:27, 30.
[4]   Isaiah 14:12–17; Ezekiel 28:12–19.
[5]   Revelation 5:11.
[6]   Psalm 78:25.
[7]   Ezekiel 1:4ff.
[8]   2 Kings 2:11.
[9]   2 Kings 6:17.
[10] Ephesians 6:12.
[11] Daniel 10:13.
[12] Isaiah 14:12.
[13] Luke 1:19.
[14] Implied from the text.
[15] Implied from Ephesians 2:2.
[16] Implied from Zephaniah 3:17.
[17] Ezekiel 28:15.
[18] 2 Corinthians 11:14.
[19] Ezekiel 28:13–15 (MSG).
[20] Jude 6.
[21] Genesis 1:2.
[22] Genesis 1:31.
[23] Dr. Edward A Boudreaux and Eric C Baxter, *God Created the Earth* (Littleton, CO: Rocky Mountain Creation Fellowship, 2009).

[24] Additional geological evidence has resulted from the Mount Saint Helen's volcanic eruption on May 18, 1980; see www.answersingenesis.org/geology/mount-st-helens/.

[25] Genesis 1:27.

[26] Hebrews 2:7.

[27] Genesis 1:28.

[28] Romans 6:16.

[29] John 3:16–18.

[30] Luke 10:19.

Chapter 2: The Creator

[1] Exodus 3:14.

[2] Romans 1:19–20.

[3] Genesis 1:1.

[4] Boudreaux and Baxter, *God Created the Earth*.

Chapter 3: Pilot Torture

[1] John 10:34–36.

[2] John 6:68–69.

[3] The Epic of Gilgamesh is a poem that comes from ancient Mesopotamia ca 2100 BCE.

[4] Bill Maher trashes the Bible on his TV programs.

[5] Exodus 14:21–28.

[6] Exodus 14:2.

Chapter 4: Wizards and Sorcerers

[1] Genesis 1:26.

[2] Psalm 118:16.

[3] Exodus 33:23.

[4] *Howard the Duck* was a 1986 science-fiction movie from Lucasfilm and Universal Pictures.

[5] R. Laird Harris, Gleason L. Archer Jr., and Bruce K Waltke, *Theological Wordbook of the Old Testament* (Chicago: Moody Press, 1990).

[6] Exodus 33:18-19.

[7] The movie *Raiders of the Lost Ark* was released in 1981 by Paramount.

[8] Hebrews 12:29.

[9] Psalm 90:2.

10   Genesis 2:6.

11   Genesis 11:6.

12   I John 1:5.

Chapter 5: Outsmarted

1   John 1:12.

2   John 3:16, 36; Isaiah 55:1; 2 Peter 3:9; Matthew 25:46; Ezekiel 33:11.

3   Matthew 25:41.

4   Revelation 20:15.

5   Genesis 50:20.

6   Genesis 12:3.

7   Genesis 37:11.

8   Genesis 37:3–36.

9   Genesis 39:1–23.

10   Genesis 40.

Chapter 6: From Disaster Springs a Family

1   Ephesians 1:4.

2   Psalm 24:1.

3   Romans 6:16.

4   Genesis 2:17.

5   Luke 10:19; Matthew 16:19; Mark 16:17–18; 1 John 3:8; Deuteronomy 28:1–13.

6   Ephesians 2:2; 2 Corinthians 4:4; John 12:31.

7   Romans 8:22.

8   Matthew 8:26.

9   Genesis 3:8.

10   Genesis 3:14–15.

11   John 17:23.

Chapter 7: Quirks and Fickleness

1   Genesis 20:12.

2   Deuteronomy 9:6.

3   Exodus 19:8.

4   Isaiah 49:6.

5   J.R.R. Tolkien, *The Lord of the Rings Trilogy* (New York: Ballantine Books, 1937).

6   Exodus 16:28.

7   Exodus 32:23.

[8]   Exodus 32:6.

[9]   Exodus 32:33.

[10] Exodus 33:3.

[11] Numbers 16:3.

[12] Exodus 20:19.

[13] Numbers 14:22–40.

Chapter 8: Birth Paroxysms

[1]   Ephesians 1:4–5.

[2]   Genesis 3:14–15.

[3]   Numbers 11:4–6.

[4]   Genesis 12:3, 18:18, 22:18; Isaiah 42:6.

[5]   1 Samuel 15:23.

[6]   Leviticus 26:14–46.

[7]   Joshua 6:20–27.

[8]   Joshua 7:1, 11, 20–26.

[9]   Romans 11:17–18.

[10] Galatians 3.

[11] Joshua 8:1.

[12] Romans 1:18–20.

[13] Acts 10:34.

[14] Matthew 25:34.

[15] John 16:21.

Chapter 9: Fasts, Celebrations, and Sacrifices

[1]   Ephesians 2:4–6.

[2]   Esther 4:16.

[3]   Exodus 34:27–28.

[4]   Leviticus 19:18.

[5]   Matthew 22:37–40.

[6]   Ezekiel 18:20.

[7]   Leviticus 17:11.

Chapter 10: Solutions

[1]   Leviticus 23:22.

[2]   1 Kings 4:25.

[3]   Isaiah 44:24-28.

4 Genesis 48:16; Exodus 6:6; Leviticus 25:47–55, 27:9–25.

5 Hebrews 10:4–7.

6 Ezekiel 18:20; Romans 6:23.

7 Isaiah 53:6; 2 Corinthians 5:21; Romans 5:8.

8 Luke 24:31, 36–44; John 20:19–23.

9 Acts 8:26–40.

10 Colossians 1:14–17.

11 John 1:1–4, 14.

12 Matthew 4:1–10; Mark 1:12–13; Luke 4:1–13.

13 Matthew 4:3.

Chapter 11: The Missing Piece

1 Hebrews 11:19.

2 2 Corinthians 5:21.

3 Romans 8:29.

4 Numbers 23:21; Jeremiah 29:11.

5 John 3:16–17.

6 Zephaniah 3:17.

7 Romans 5:8; Ephesians 2:4-5; 1 John 4:10.

8 1 Corinthians 13.

9 Isaiah 43:16.

10 Matthew 7:11.

11 2 Chronicles 20.

12 1 Kings 17:5–14.

13 John 11:35.

14 Ezekiel 33:11.

15 Deuteronomy 9:4–6.

16 Romans 11:17–18; Galatians 3:6-9.

17 Ezekiel 37:21-28; Daniel 9:24-27

18 1 Peter 3:18–20.

19 1 Corinthians 2:9.

20 John 8:32.

Chapter 12: It's Time for an Honest Answer

1 John 5:24.

2 Romans 1:19–20.

3 Colossians 1:27.

4 1 Corinthians 6:9-11, 15–20.

5   Dr. Richard E. Eby, DO, *Caught Up into Paradise* (Old Tappan, NJ: Fleming H. Revell, 1984).

6   1 Corinthians 2:9.

7   1 John 1:9.

8   See Romans 8:29, 12:2.

Printed in the United States
By Bookmasters